SIBLINGS IN THE UNCONSCIOUS
AND PSYCHOPATHOLOGY

SIBLINGS IN THE UNCONSCIOUS AND PSYCHOPATHOLOGY

Womb Fantasies, Claustrophobias, Fear of Pregnancy, Murderous Rage, Animal Symbolism, Christmas and Easter "Neuroses", and Twinnings or Identifications with Sisters and Brothers

Vamık D. Volkan and Gabriele Ast

KARNAC

First published in 1997 by International Universities Press

This edition published in 2014 by

Karnac Books Ltd
118 Finchley Road
London NW3 5HT

British Library Cataloguing in Publication Data
A C.I.P. for this book is available from the British Library

ISBN: 978-178220-161-8

Printed in Great Britain
www.karnacbooks.com

To our sisters, Tomris Güney and Sevim Kuzey of the Turkish Republic of Northern Cyprus, Hanni Markovitis of Greece, and Christine Gatz of Germany, with love.

CONTENTS

ACKNOWLEDGMENTS

Drs. Gabriele Ast and Vamık Volkan previously coauthored two books, *Eine Borderline Therapie* and *Spektrum des Narzißmus*, which were published in Germany. This is our first jointly written work in English. We hope that the input from clinical observations from two countries, Germany and the United States, enriches our work.

We thank Dr. William Greer, Ph.D., of Hampton, Virginia and Eli Zaller, M.D., of Richmond, Virginia for giving us permission to report their cases of Mary and Christine, respectively. Dr. Greer also helped in the writing of his case.

INTRODUCTION

This book examines the mental representations of childhood siblings as influential object representations or identifications in adult patients' internal worlds, and the role they play in psychopathology. Intrapsychic experiences with such representations, contaminated with unconscious fantasies and affects, can be key elements in the formation or maintenance of symptoms or personality traits.

The role of childhood sibling representations in the intrapsychic experiences of *adults*, whether it leads to positive (adaptive) or negative (psychopathological) outcomes, in its own right, has not received a systematic investigation in the psychoanalytic literature. The literature on sibling representations in *children's* inner worlds is more available. However, child psychoanalysts mostly write about the easily observable manifestations of childhood sibling experiences, not about the long-term intrapsychic consequences of such experiences. For example, rivalry for parental attention, children's reactions to a sibling birth or death, and having a twin or a sick sister or brother are mentioned frequently.

When child psychoanalysts turn their attention to the role of sibling representations in separation-individuation, oedipal, latency, and adolescent passage issues, they do not usually give it primary consideration. One reason for this is that the representations of mother, father, and other caregivers take center stage in the consideration of developmental issues. In the writings of child psychoanalysts the important adults' representations in a child's mind tend to contaminate and overshadow the representations of siblings, with a few notable exceptions. Leichtman (1985), for example, argues that elder children themselves influence the separation–individuation process of their younger siblings. Graham (1988) reaches the conclusion that there is a separate line of separation-individuation from earliest childhood which relates to sibling experiences and "which operates along and/or is intricately linked with infantile attachments to and separations from both parents" (p. 107). Sharpe and Rosenblatt (1994) believe that "Sibling [oedipal] triangles exist independent of parent–child triangles and undergo parallel development into constellations bearing significant formal and dynamic similarities to the standard parent–child oedipal relationships" (p. 491).

Child psychoanalysts also have provided detailed cases of children and their psychoanalytic treatments, and these cases illustrate the influence of childhood sibling experiences in the evolution of defenses, adaptations, and personality traits. Kennedy (1985), for example, reports on David, who was not quite 12 years old when he started analysis. David grew up with a handicapped brother who was seven years older. Since the parents expected their older son's early death, David also served as a kind of "replacement child" (Cain and Cain, 1964; Poznanski, 1972). Furthermore, he experienced a sibling loss at the age of 8 when his afflicted brother died.

Kennedy shows that David's defenses against wishing his brother dead extended to a generalized condemnation of his own aggression. This, in turn, made him incapable of self-assertion. His restriction on aggressive expression led to a strong reaction formation, talion fears, and a strict superego. David also identified with his sick brother's mental representation in order to receive his mother's love. But this identification mobilized fears that he too might suffer the older brother's fate and die. His problems dealing with aggression made it difficult for David to negotiate the oedipal issues.

Kennedy's report on childhood sibling experiences and defensive responses is not an isolated one. We specifically chose to refer to her work, though, for the following reason: after nearly three years of working with David and after apparently helping him a great deal, Kennedy has lingering concerns about him. She finishes her report on this case with some questions—the very kinds of questions that we try to answer in this book. She writes:

> It is, of course, impossible to predict the future of this child [David]. Will he succumb to hypochondriacal symptoms or concerns? Will he be vulnerable to pervasive anxieties, especially those connected with illness or death? Will his relationships in his own future family be put in jeopardy and echo some of the miseries encountered in the past? Or will compassion and the character traits already well established lead to a medical career, the caring profession, a future defender of the needy, or a crusader for the handicapped? [p. 273].

Kennedy, in writing about David's childhood, wonders how the experience of growing up with a handicapped sibling will "settle in" to his adult internal world. In our book, as psychoanalysts of adults, we analyze adults' internal worlds in order to illustrate the fate of childhood sibling experiences and their pathological influences. We try to answer the underlying question: How does the adult's mental representation of a sibling evolve from that which he or she formed in childhood? Under "normal" conditions, the adult would continue to relate to the sibling in the external world, resulting in modifications to the mental representation of the sibling over time. The cathexis of the mental representation would increase or decrease according to the adult's internal need to link himself or herself to the sibling. Normally the adult will also identify with aspects of the sibling's representation for the rest of his or her life and then adapt internally to those identifications in ways that do not result in disturbing symptoms or personality traits. Identification with the sibling's representation would paradoxically provide a separation and individuation from the sibling and the sibling's representation. However, if there is an unfinished sexual, aggressive, or object relations conflict with the sibling's representation, it remains an influential object representation and identification with it becomes problematic, sometimes demanding the continual attention of the adult's mind.

Our experience with adult patients shows us that representations of siblings influence separation-individuation, oedipal, and other developmental issues, and that these influences are usually contaminated with the dominant role played by parents' representations in these areas. But sibling experiences, in their own right, become key elements in an adult's psychic life when they are included in specific unconscious fantasies. In an adult's mind these unconscious fantasies can catapult sibling representations to primary roles in creating durable symptoms as well as pathological personality traits. When this happens the analysis of such an adult needs to focus initially on the unconscious sibling experiences, since they, like black holes in space, absorb the surrounding developmental issues. Such developmental issues cannot be analyzed until the unconscious sibling experiences—the influence of representations of siblings contaminated with unconscious fantasies—have been understood and worked through. In order to illustrate this theoretical position we include here an abundance of clinical illustrations. We believe the strength of this volume lies in our presentation of cases and our dependence on them for support of our theoretical formulations.

Since this book focuses on siblings' representations in the unconscious, especially their role as "actors or actresses" in unconscious fantasy stories, in the first chapter we begin by explaining what we mean by unconscious fantasies.

1 UNCONSCIOUS FANTASIES

Our own experiences make us familiar with *conscious fantasies* or daydreams: stories in our minds that gratify our narcissistic or object-seeking and sexual or aggressive wishes. In our conscious fantasies we make ourselves princes or princesses, we take revenge on our enemies, or conquer sexually desirable partners. Other conscious fantasies are masochistic in nature; they satisfy unconscious wishes to submit to the demands of harsh superegos. Some conscious fantasies, whether they aim to temporarily increase our self-esteem or devalue or punish ourselves, end with masturbation: a bodily discharge to relieve tensions associated with closeness or distance to objects and to satisfy various aspects of infantile sexuality and infantile aggression. While it is easy to understand and explain conscious fantasies (daydreams) theoretically, the metapsychological formulations about *unconscious fantasies* have been rather difficult. First of all, patients do not directly report their unconscious fantasies. As Beres (1962) suggested, we surmise the existence of an unconscious fantasy "from the effects it produces, as the physicist surmises the existence of the electrical particles of atoms by the effects they produce" (p. 309). The story lines of unconscious fantasies are not presented in words and sentences. The patient, with the help of the analyst, *reconstructs* the story lines of unconscious fantasies during analytic treatment.

1

Once the story line of an unconscious fantasy is put into language, we often see that its aim resembles a conscious daydream: it may serve to restore the person's lowered self-esteem or satisfy sexual and aggressive demands, narcissistic or object-seeking wishes, or submissions to or rebellion against the superego or superego forerunners (i.e., "bad" object representations). But, as we will soon describe, before reconstructing the unconscious fantasy and putting its story line into language, we must recognize how it differs from conscious daydreams and fantasies in relation to its role in the person's mind, its level of organization, and its resistance to modification.

Conscious daydreams are influenced by the secondary process type of thinking—even the surface picture may appear illogical. For example, a child daydreams of having an imaginary companion, a "bad" twin, while in reality she is an only child. Once the symbolic meaning of the imaginary companion is understood, namely, as a displacement figure for the child's vices such as selfishness, envy, or uncleanliness or for responding to the child's feelings of emptiness, neglect, or rejection (Freiberg, 1959; Nagera, 1969), the meaning and function of the daydream is easily explainable. Unlike conscious daydreams the "stories" of unconscious fantasies are based on the primary process type of thinking: they remain illogical so far as the adult mind is concerned, even after their story lines are put into language. They are differentiated "from other varieties of unconscious content by their enduring quality and their organized, story-like quality reflecting the distortions typical of the primary process. As dynamically unconscious templates from the childhood past, they shape subsequent compromise formations and are relatively impervious to new experience" (Inderbitzin and Levy, 1990, p. 113). Furthermore, conscious daydreams differ from unconscious fantasies in that the patient realizes the involvement of his imaginative process in the former but perceives the latter as reality (Schafer, 1968).

In practice, however, once an unconscious fantasy is reconstructed in the analytic treatment, it may be difficult to make a differentiation between the story line of an unconscious fantasy and the story line of a daydream, and to differentiate their functions in the person's internal world. Furthermore, while conscious fantasies, because the patient recognizes their imaginative aspects, are relatively straightforward to analyze and treat, the modification of the "reality" of the unconscious fantasy in treatment proves to be more difficult.

Themes concerning the primal scene, incest, beating, castration, bisexuality, phallic women, rescue, oedipal urges, and family romance frequently appear in unconscious fantasies. These are common themes that, because all humans share similar psychophysiological early life experiences, are almost universal. We may assume that many elements of unconscious fantasy life, as well as daydreams, that contain these themes are shared cross-culturally (Moore and Fine, 1990). In this book we focus on pregnancy, birth, and sibling themes.

Ever since the early writings of Freud (1900, 1905a,b, 1908a, 1909a,b, 1911, 1915), the concept of unconscious fantasies has been addressed in psychoanalytic literature. During the last few decades significant papers on unconscious fantasies have been written by Beres (1962), Sandler and Nagera (1963), Arlow (1969a, b), Slap and Saykin (1983), Sandler and Sandler (1986), Sandler (1986), Apprey (1987), Blum, Kramer, Richards and Richards (1988), Abend (1990), Dowling (1990), Inderbitzin and Levy (1990), Shane and Shane (1990), and Trossman (1990). Yet in spite of the abundance of scholarly reports on the unconscious fantasy, as Sandler and Sandler (1986) and Inderbitzin and Levy (1990) state, the concept remains elastic or unclear, having "a range of meanings, incapable of precise definition" (Sandler and Sandler, 1986, p. 109). Melanie Klein and her followers (Klein, 1948; Isaacs, 1948; Segal, 1973) maintain that unconscious "phantasies" (Kleinian spelling) are inherited; they explain that they begin as psychic representations of instincts (drives) and may subsequently become elaborated into well-formed wishes or defenses against anxiety. Kleinians say that since drives are present at birth, some crude fantasy life can be assumed as existing at birth. For example, Segal (1973) states: "The first hunger and the instinctual striving to satisfy that hunger are accompanied by the phantasy of an object capable of satisfying that hunger. As phantasies derive directly from instincts on the borderline between the somatic and psychical activity, these original phantasies are experienced as somatic as well as mental phenomena" (p. 13).

Freud (1908b) stated that "Unconscious phantasies have either been unconscious all along and have been formed in the unconscious; or—as is more often the case—they were once conscious phantasies, day-dreams, and have since been purposely forgotten and have become unconscious through 'repression'" (p. 161). In this book we use the concept of unconscious fantasy in a more restricted sense, similar to Freud's second explanation of this phenomenon—that they are repressed daydreams, or more precisely, they are repressed "interpretations" of a child's experience of a traumatic event. We agree with Moore and Fine (1990) in that a description of the unconscious fantasy must incorporate experiences and memories.

A child perceives, comprehends, and "interprets" a traumatic event—whether it happens once or is repeated, such as a mother's repeated inability to respond to the child's developmental needs—which, due to its psychological significance, induces a strong emotion in him. His "interpretation" depends upon his cognitive capacities, the developmental (i.e., psychosexual, aggressive) and self and object relations issues he is negotiating at the time, and the level of emotion the event initiates. The child's "interpretation" of an event or repeated events is also influenced by those intimate persons in his environment. For example, the mother's own perception and affects about an event may make the child more or less anxious in experiencing it. Furthermore, mothers and important others have their own unconscious fantasies, and under certain circumstances they pass them on to their offspring who then develop unconscious responses to them, including unconscious fantasies (Apprey, 1993). Volkan and Masri (1989) examined a teenage female transsexual and her parents. The patient's mother had traumatized her baby daughter by repeatedly physically manipulating the child's genitalia. The mother, who was depressed and sexually "hungry," unconsciously perceived her daughter as a penis and often slept with the infant between her legs, thinking of her as a "Martian" who, like a penis, should not be exhibited in public. The transsexual's father had a deformity in his mouth which was corrected by plastic surgery. In the girl's development of female transsexualism and her seeking surgical help to have a "penis" constructed for her, we see the combined effects of the mother's unconscious fantasy of a baby/penis equation, the father's conscious belief that surgery can correct one's body image, and the girl's corresponding "interpretations" of the traumatic events of her childhood.

For the child's "interpretation" to be an unconscious fantasy it has to be repressed and be influenced and distorted by the primary process thinking. When this happens, as unconscious "contents," it exerts a never-ending dynamic effect on subsequent perceptions, behavior, thinking, responses to reality, and either adaptive or maladaptive compromise formations (Arlow, 1969a,b; Inderbitzin and Levy, 1990). The child's developmental level at the time of his "interpretation" of the traumatic event influences the nature of the unconscious fantasy. For example, if he is at the oral phase and experiences an important figure as a "bad" object he may develop illogical ways of annihilating the representations of this object, such as by eating it; if he is subjected to a primal scene when at the anal phase and the experience induces strong emotions in him, his understanding of the event may include a fantasy of anal intercourse and anal impregnation. The difficulty with these examples, however, is that they depend upon the idea that a few-months-old baby can have a "formed" thought of killing someone by eating her or that a toddler can have a "formed" thought of anal impregnation, and that later they repress these structured ideations. We do not believe in the existence of well-developed thoughts, however illogical they might be, in infancy and in early childhood. Instead, the infant and the very young child experience somatic, affective, and cognitive responses to a trauma and later they are repressed. Here, we are interested in the combination of these responses having the potential to create a story line for an unconscious fantasy once such responses are re-activated. Very early in life the combination of these responses do not generate formed and sustainable thoughts until later, when they are re-activated and get connected to formed thoughts.

We must ask what happens if the somatic, affective, and cognitive responses do *not* lead to the formation of an unconscious fantasy. We believe that under such conditions the responses to the trauma may lead to psychosomatic expressions later in life.

In other words, we are theorizing that there is an interplay between the formation and maintenance of unconscious fantasies
and psychosomatic expressions. The latter relate to the most
primitive channel of discharging responses to trauma, especially
affects. Unconscious fantasies, on the other hand, are the first
mental channels to express and master them. If later in life the
mastery of the trauma via unconscious fantasies become "threatened," the individual may resort to the utilization of psychosomatic channels. The reverse is also true: if the unconscious
fantasies are not blocked and thus remain effective, they may
prevent the initiation of psychosomatic expressions.

The function of unconscious fantasies can be threatened by
various circumstances. This might occur when events in the individual's environment suddenly match the elements of the story
line in his unconscious fantasy, and the individual experiences
this as though his fantasy has become "real." Now the "merging"
of external reality with "psychic reality" threatens the function
of the unconscious fantasy. For example, imagine a man who has
an unconscious fantasy of entering his mother's belly to kill his
younger sibling there. In reality, let us say, this man enacts his
unconscious fantasy by becoming an explorer of caves, where the
caves represent the mother's womb, and his exploration represents his search for his sibling in order to murder him. As long
as he finds no one in the caves, his spelunking activities serve as
a defense against his own aggression. However, after a period of
time his aggression builds up and he must again explore caves.
The activity of exploring but not finding anyone continues to
maintain his unconscious defense against aggression. Then one
day the man happens upon a dead body in a cave. Now reality
too closely matches his unconscious fantasy, his unconscious strat-
egy of defense fails, and he may regress to expressing his feelings—feelings of rejection by his mother when the sibling was
born–psychosomatically.

Another circumstance that threatens the function of the unconscious fantasy occurs during psychoanalysis. Psychosomatic
symptoms may appear, if only temporarily, when therapeutic
progress uncovers the story line of the unconscious fantasy which
the patient now recognizes as such. Thus the previous effectiveness of unconscious fantasy changes. In the description of our

clinical work with patients Mira (see chapter 6) and Gisela (see chapter 10), we further illustrate the interplay between the effective maintenance of unconscious fantasies and the expression of psychosomatic symptoms when the function of the unconscious fantasy is threatened.

We must also ask another question. What happens if the infant's or very young child's initial responses to his "interpretation" of the trauma do not get repressed? In this situation the child's responses may later become elements on which a conscious fantasy can be built. The individual, however, eventually will recognize the imaginary process (Schafer, 1968) in the conscious fantasy (which includes a function to gratify one or another kind of wish). The conscious fantasy, unlike the unconscious fantasy, does not become a stubborn psychic reality.

If a traumatic event occurs *later* in life when the child has a better ability for perception and thinking and is better able to tame affects, he may form a structured explanation (a formal and sustainable thought) for the trauma, but even this explanation is illogical from an adult's point of view. This well-formed "interpretation" then may be repressed and become an unconscious fantasy. It is necessary for us to visualize a hierarchy in the formation of unconscious fantasies that corresponds to a child's age and ego development.

A grown-up child, furthermore, may "reinterpret" a traumatic event when a similar event occurs in reality later on. On the conscious level the child's previous understanding of the event may be modified. The new and more reality-oriented "interpretation" may become an ally to the ego function in more strongly maintaining the repression of the first "understanding," rendering the first "understanding" less influential or less harmful. However, to explain the existence of unconscious fantasies we must consider situations in which the first "interpretation" is not given up at all, is not rendered harmless, but instead stays there like an inner and alive "fossil." It absorbs sexual and aggressive wishes, object-relation issues, and either defensive or adaptive measures against anxiety, and mixes them up with primary process ideas and images. Since it resides in the unconscious, we refer to it as an unconscious fantasy. We agree with Sandler and Sandler (1986) that an unconscious fantasy, as described above, "deserves the name of fantasy only inasmuch as [it is] *derived* from the contents of conscious or preconscious fantasies" (p. 111). In turn, unconscious fantasies, as the Sandlers state, find expression in new conscious and preconscious daydreams.

Our description of unconscious fantasy especially echoes Arlow's (1969b) remarks. He states:

> [I]n keeping with the synthetic function of the ego and the principle of multiple function, the traumatic events in the individual's life and the pathogenic conflicts that grow out of them are worked over defensively by the ego and incorporated into a scheme of memories and patterns of fantasy. In one part of the mind, the inner eye, as it were, remains focused on an inner stream of fantasy thought in which the traumatic memories are retained in disguised form. . . . The traumatic events of the past become part of the fantasy thinking and as such exert a never-ending dynamic effect, occasionally striking, sometimes less so, on our responses to and appreciation of reality [pp. 43–44].

THE EFFECT OF SIBLINGS ON UNCONSCIOUS FANTASIES

Let us start with a child who has a younger sibling; according to his age and stage of developmental issues, the child develops images and collections of images (mental representations) of the younger sibling even before the baby is born. He collects data about the rival. The mother's remarks about her pregnancy and unborn child, the mother's affects about the same, the child's perception of his mother's morning sickness and growing belly, the child's touching his mother's abdomen and feeling the unborn child, and other related events allow the child to form images and mental representations of the new arrival and he mixes them up with expectations (i.e., the fear of losing the mother's love). Because of real deprivations (e.g., the mother's having a postpartum depression and not being available enough to the older child) and because of the older child's internal processes (e.g., identification with the depressed mother), the sibling experience may prove traumatic. The more traumatic it is the more likely the older child will contaminate his experience with complicated perceptions, thoughts, expectations, and feelings. As these get repressed they become included in an unconscious fantasy dominated by primary processes.

The most common theme of the child's unconscious sibling fantasies concerns the image of the new sibling in the mother's belly and the older child's wishes about what to do with it. The older child, for example, in his unconscious fantasy enters the mother's womb or belly in order to get rid of the rival. In his fantasy he owns his mother's belly and no one but he can occupy it.

It goes without saying that younger children also have unconscious fantasies that include the mental representations of their older siblings. However, in our experience in analyzing adults, we could not find the existence of womb fantasies among last-born children. If such unconscious fantasies among that population exist we would not be surprised, however, because the youngest child's territoriality too may be threatened—and so the younger child may wish for the safety and comfort of the womb. In our experience the youngest child's unconscious fantasies pertaining to elder siblings occur more often when the former has experienced a trauma such as being threatened or beaten by the older child, or experiencing the older child's illness or death. The death of an older sibling, for example, may occur during a time when the younger child has severe castration anxiety. In turn, the younger child unconsciously equates death with castration, and then "interprets" the loss of the older child as the loss of the penis. The younger child keeps the mental representation of the dead sibling (a penis) "alive" in his mind as a defense against castration.

The other common unconscious fantasies among younger children relate to their being replacements for dead siblings. Here, too, the mother or parents' attitude toward the newborn child plays an important role in his development of an unconscious "story" that he exists to replace a dead older child whom, often, he has never met. For a child to have an unconscious fantasy that he replaces or "is" another person (who is dead, and who may belong to the opposite sex) may induce fragmentation in his self representation and cause conflicted self and object relations and even gender conflicts. A related unconscious fantasy is that one has to die for another one to live (Apprey, 1987). When we present detailed case material in later chapters we will demonstrate how these and other unconscious fantasies related to sibling experiences can be reconstructed in psychoanalysis.

In the next chapter we begin studying the *older* child's reactions to a new sibling and the internalized consequences of those reactions in adulthood. We examine how the new sibling is perceived as an "intruder" in the older child's psychic and physical space. We provide examples of certain common clinical observations of adults in analysis to illustrate how their internal worlds can be understood through the examination of the "intruder's" representation associated with affects, unconscious fantasies, defenses, and adaptations.

2 THE INTRUDER

Child psychoanalyst Parens (1980) describes a mother's pregnancy and sibling's birth as "average, expectable events" (p. 419) which disturb the existing equilibrium for the older child, but do so only temporarily; in a healthy environment a new equilibrium is then established and the experience is not traumatic. Nevertheless the older child begins to experience, to one degree or another, sibling rivalry. Used loosely, the term *sibling rivalry*, indicating a feeling of competition for the mother's attention, has come to carry a negative connotation (Levy, 1937). This does not mean, however, that Freud and other analysts have not also acknowledged the *positive* aspects of the mother's pregnancy, sibling birth, and early sibling experience. We, too, have observed both positive and negative consequences of sibling experiences. But since this book focuses on psychopathology, in this chapter we begin to examine the reasons why in some cases "average, expectable events" become traumatic and how their influence appears in adults.

THE NEW BABY AS AN INTRUDER

When a baby enters the family circle, she enters both the physical *and* the psychological territory of the older sibling, causing a change and imposing a "sense of object loss" (Parens, 1980, p. 419) in the older child's existing frame of reference. This change requires the older child to make an external, and more importantly, an internal, adaptation to the new situation. The child's age, her developmental status, the nature of the parent–child relationship, and certain cultural influences determine how she will experience, "interpret," and internalize the mother's pregnancy and the intrusion of a new baby into her physical and psychic space. Solnit (1983) states "Whether expressed in rivalry or cooperation with, envy or admiration of, or by affection or hatred for the sibling, the nature of the parent–child relationship and the child's developmental level are two major intersecting axes along which to gauge and understand the quality of the sibling experience" (p. 283). In this chapter, besides describing these two axes, we have addressed certain cultural–religious influences that affect the two axes.

According to the child's internal circumstances and the external conditions, the baby's arrival may initiate one or more of the four expectations that signal danger as outlined by Freud (1926): the loss of mother, the loss of mother's love, castration, and the loss of self-esteem. A child at the oral level (or an older child who regresses to the oral level) may perceive that the mother gives her love away piecemeal, feeling, "if one piece of the pie goes to the baby then there will be less for me!" This perception, and the unconscious fantasy pertaining to it, occurs through a psychological process that was described in the previous chapter. A child at the anal phase or regressing to that level may equate the baby with feces (Freud, 1908b). She may retain the stool (Mahler, 1966) as if not letting go of the feces equates to not allowing the birth of the sibling to take place. In developing this constipation the anal child identifies with the pregnant mother.

The experience of the mother's pregnancy and a sibling's birth influences the nature of the Oedipus complex; Freud offered an example of this in the case of Little Hans (Freud, 1909a). A boy in the oedipal years may unconsciously perceive the new baby as a product of love between him and his mother, or as the extension of the rival, his father. A girl in the oedipal years may unconsciously wish that the baby belongs to her and her father, an idea which intensifies her rivalry with her mother and carries with it accompanying psychological implications. Colonna and Newman (1983) state that, "The degree to which a girl's penis envy and a boy's castration anxiety is intensified by the birth of an opposite-sexed sibling during the phallic phase is a well-accepted clinical finding" (p. 296). Adolescent passage (Blos, 1979), with its developmental turmoil, presents another arena where the mother's pregnancy and the sibling's birth may act as a traumatic stimulant if internal or external conditions disturb the child's reaction to these "average, expectable events."

The parents' conscious and unconscious view of the new baby and the nature of their emotional support for the older sibling also influence the way the older child experiences and internalizes the mother's pregnancy and the arrival of the new baby. The older sibling, like Freud's (1909a) Little Hans, may openly protest the usurpation of her first-class status. The reactions may manifest themselves in new symptoms or easily observable personality traits, including intensification of oral–sadistic impulses, sleeping and eating problems, and phobias (Freud, 1909a; Bornstein, 1949; Sperling, 1952; Lundberg, 1979), increased fantasy role play (Ritvo and Solnit, 1958), creating imaginary companions (Freiberg, 1959; Nagera, 1969), fear of death (Bornstein, 1953), constipation (Mahler, 1966), wetting, clinging, increased sensitivity to incidents of physical hurt (Novick, 1974), and so on.

Symptoms and easily detected personality traits may be only the tip of an iceberg and may not reveal the full and sometimes lifelong impact of certain unconscious reactions and hidden personality traits. For example, the child may partly identify in a disruptive way with the new sibling's mental representation. Since this takes place unconsciously she does not know of the identification and does not complain of its consequences. This disruptive identification belongs to the submerged part of the iceberg. The identification is in the service of defending herself against losing mother or her love—or even against castration or losing self-esteem. In other words, if she is similar to or the same as her sibling she will receive the part of the mother's love directed toward the new sibling. This kind of identification may have a negative impact on the older child throughout her life.

DISRUPTIVE IDENTIFICATION WITH A YOUNGER SIBLING

The case of Chris Albert, a physician, illustrates such a disruptive identification process and its impact in adulthood. His total case and psychoanalytic treatment process have been published (Volkan, 1984). Here we report only the material from his case relevant to the topic of this book.

When Dr. Albert was 4 years old, and experiencing heightened oedipal wishes for his mother, his younger brother was born. In Dr. Albert's early years his mother sometimes acted toward him in a way that was openly seductive, making her son's attachment to her intense. Therefore, he experienced his mother's pregnancy and the birth of a brother as very traumatic. When he began his analysis he could not remember his mother's pregnancy or his brother's birth. While he had no conscious memory of these events, he expressed his reaction to the birth and to his early sibling experience in the flawed memory of a straw hat. Dr. Albert had a vivid recollection of wearing a straw hat as a child, and he recounted the following story to his analyst. According to Dr. Albert, as a child he had a thymus problem, and he received the customary cure for it of the time—radiation treatments. The family physician warned his mother to protect her child from the sun's rays because the extra radiation would hurt him. So the mother bought a straw hat, and little Chris Albert wore it whenever in the sun. In his mind's eye he could see himself as a child hiding from the sunlight under the straw hat, which he knew protected him from becoming ill.

In his adult life Dr. Albert had a personality trait of being overly cautious, and he was usually unaware of it. He acted as though one wrong step, in either his professional or his home life, could, like exposure to sunlight, prove dangerous. One can imagine Dr. Albert's surprise when in the third year of his analysis, his therapeutic work enabled him to realize that it was not *he* who had worn the straw hat, but his younger brother! His mother and an examination of his and his brother's medical records verified this discovery. The records indicated that Albert had received just *one* session of radiation therapy at 4 months old, while his brother had undergone repeated treatments and had worn the protective straw hat. His having had one treatment, we suspect, provided a kernel of truth in his belief that he had a childhood illness, but in fact, it was his brother who had been truly sick. By identifying with a sick brother's representation, Dr. Albert had attempted to recapture his mother's love. The consequences of this identification was his remaining overly cautious as an adult. His unconscious fantasy was that the sun would melt him and then he would lose his mother. The straw hat, like the shadow of his mother, would protect him and thus not only would he continue to live, but he would continue to have his mother's attention. The straw hat, at one level, represented his mother's protective body next to his body. This fantasy also was connected with oedipal issues. As an adult he distanced himself from the oedipal father (the sun) and tried to remain in the shadow of the oedipal mother (straw hat).

YOUNGER SIBLING AS AN INFLUENTIAL OBJECT REPRESENTATION

Dr. Albert had identified totally with his younger brother's "sick child" representation when he believed that he (Dr. Albert) was the one who wore the straw hat. But the older child's interactions with the representation of the younger sibling does not always lead to an identification. Sometimes the younger sibling's representation becomes symbolized as a wished-for or dreaded object and remains as an influential object representation in the adult's mind.

A 30-year-old woman in analysis, Jennifer, stated that she feared pregnancy and childbirth because they would deform her body. Underneath her fears lay a symbolization of her younger sibling's representation and a phallus/baby equation. Her father was a gynecologist who used to drink excessively on the weekends. When drunk he sometimes acted seductively toward his daughter and sometimes did things that scared her. He loved guns and in a drunken state he would shoot his guns, sometimes in the house, scaring the little girl. She wanted to become his loving darling, but because she feared him she attempted to "join him" in identification, a form of identification with the aggressor (A. Freud, 1936), in order to ease her anxiety. This in turn increased her unconscious wish to have a penis.

The older of two children, Jennifer had experienced the arrival of her sibling at the age of 3, and she associated her sibling with a wished-for penis she could share with her father. Her unconscious baby/penis fantasy crystallized when she secretly watched, at the oedipal age, her gynecologist father examining pregnant women. When these women delivered their babies, the child heard the mothers scream since her father's clinic was located next door to the family home. She attributed their screams to the removal of their penises (babies) by her father. He would not share them with his daughter, however, leaving her frustrated.

She grew up to be a very attractive woman. But beneath her feminine appearance she kept searching for her sibling/penis. It was her denial of this search and her anxiety that her "penis" would be removed in a gynecological clinic that made her fear pregnancy and childbirth.

During a period of her analysis this patient spent considerable time in a stable watching the delivery of foals in order to modify the influence of her unconscious fantasy pertaining to the representation of her sibling. Until the meaning of her visits to the stable was interpreted in analysis, she was unconscious of the function of this compulsion. Even after becoming conscious of it, she still expected the mare to deliver a penis. Fortunately, seeing multiple deliveries, along with further work on her interest in the delivery of foals, increased her reality testing and modified the effect of her unconscious fantasy.

CHRISTMAS AND EASTER "NEUROSES"

Besides individualized disruptive identifications with the representations of younger siblings or reactions to them as influential object representations, there are unconscious fantasies attached to the representations of younger brothers and sisters which lead to difficulties in adulthood. Some of these difficulties are shared by many. An unconscious fantasy equating Christ with a new sibling can be found in a type of "neurosis" which occurs mostly among individuals from Christian cultures. It coincides with Christian religious holidays and is thus called "Christmas neurosis" or "Easter neurosis" accordingly.

Many clinicians have observed that some individuals react negatively to holidays, especially Christmas and Easter. Explanations for this "neurosis" have varied according to the specific psychodynamics exhibited by the individual during analysis. Freud (1918) described the Wolf Man's frustration that he did not receive as many presents as he felt he deserved; and since Christmas day coincided roughly with the Wolf Man's birthday, he made an identification with Christ and expected a masochistic relationship with his father/God. Jekels (1936) saw traces of the Oedipus complex in the Christmas "neurosis." He stated that it encourages a false sense of equality between the son and his father causing intrapsychic problems and anxiety. Eisenbud (1941) reports on two women who had unresolved competitive feelings with a male sibling. These two women suffered from intense penis envy and became depressed at Christmastime when their renewed childhood hope that Santa Claus would bring them phalluses was dashed once again.

It was Boyer (1955) who made a systematic study of the relationship between the Christmas story and childbirth and presented clinical material from twenty-one patients; later (1985) he reported findings from work with an additional fifty patients. All of the seventy-one patients were either analyzed by Boyer or in psychoanalytic psychotherapy with him. All of these individuals regressed and exhibited depressive reactions during the Christmas season. Some of them became blatantly psychotic in the consultation room.

Boyer indicates that Christmas "neurosis" is not a true form of neurosis, but signifies instead the reactivation of unresolved feelings about the birth of a sibling during a time when the birth of Christ becomes a prominent cultural theme. The individual then gets involved in an internal and conflictual relationship with the mental representation of her sibling. Her aggression intensifies in this relationship, and when she turns the aggression toward herself, this lowers self-esteem, which generates depression or fear of annihilation. As the new sibling, Christ presents a rival with whom these depression-prone individuals cannot compete. The season reawakens real or imagined failures to cope with siblings. Boyer mentions intensification of oral conflicts, repressed cravings, and frustrations as reactions to Christmas.

CULTURAL INFLUENCES

Christmas "neurosis" illustrates how reactions to a new sibling, as influenced by other developmental issues, find expression in a culturally shared "neurosis." The culture we live in changes the observable expression of the sibling experience, while many unconscious psychodynamic processes pertaining to such experiences remain similar. The influences of cultural customs and traditions appear more clearly in homogenous communities relatively uncontaminated by complex interactions with other groups. Once more we turn to the work of Boyer to explore cultural impact on sibling representations.

Boyer's (1979) psychoanalytic study of the Apache personality refers to behavior patterns which reflect insecurely repressed traumatic sibling experiences. Typically, an Apache woman of child-bearing age in an Apache community will bear her second child less than two years after her first. At the time of the second child's birth, the parents *abruptly* remove the older child from their bed or from his cradle. The mother's attention focuses on the new baby, inducing a severe "rapprochement crisis" in the displaced child (Mahler, Pine, and Bergman, 1975). The displaced child, due to the stage of his muscular and psychosexual maturation, needs to learn self-control and control over his emotions so that he can fit into society. He does not receive the necessary help, however, from his parents.

Among Apaches the toddler's overt expression of hostility toward the new sibling is taboo, and when it occurs provokes adult ridicule. However, Boyer observes, when a last-born is present, the displaced toddler discovers that he may attack *older* siblings or destroy their property with impunity, even with the parents about. In this tacitly approved displacement, the child turns his rage against the last-born toward the older siblings. Furthermore, the displaced child is encouraged to torment pets, such as puppies. Unsurprisingly, Apaches fear being bitten by the neighbors' dogs. Their reaction to dogs also appears in their ambivalence toward the coyote, the trickster character who alternates between wise man and clown. Boyer speaks of "institutionalized phobias" (p. 62) in which group-encouraged phobias serve to absorb the sibling rivalry which cannot be completely repressed or handled by reaction formations. He goes on to describe what happens to the Apache child developmentally beyond the rapprochement crises, and he illustrates the effects of insecurely repressed feelings about siblings in the adult Apache. Boyer notes, for example, that many Apaches, when intoxicated, are unusually brutal toward sibling surrogates.

Psychoanalytic anthropologist Kracke (1978) reports on the Kagwahiv Indians of Brazil. The customs and beliefs of this culture also play a role in intensifying sibling rivalry. Kagwahiv mothers regard their newborn babies as very delicate. The mothers prefer to keep nursing them until they voluntarily give up the breast. However, the Kagwahiv also believe that if two children nurse from the same mother or even take powdered milk from the same can, it will "poison" the milk. Since the Kagwahiv mother, like the Apache mother, most likely will have another child within a few years, the older child will necessarily undergo an abrupt weaning. This disrupts the toddler's physical and emotional territory, leading to intensified sibling rivalry. The Kagwahiv mothers, aware of the conflict between the children, severely reprimand any expression of sibling rivalry, which further complicates matters for the displaced child. Kracke also observes that a reflection of this suppressed aggressive behavior gets directed against fellow group members later in life.

3 INSECTS, FISH, BIRDS, AND ANIMALS

In the previous chapters we wrote about the individual's internalized relationship with the representations of siblings. This chapter examines how sibling representations frequently appear in symbolized form. In *The Interpretation of Dreams,* early in the psychoanalytic movement, Freud (1900) referred to hostility between siblings as playing a primary role in the establishment of psychopathology. Freud illustrated how in "typical dreams" unconscious feelings toward a sibling may appear as the death of someone beloved or as the appearance of the sibling in the form of vermin or a small animal. Freud wrote that in dreams "being plagued with vermin is often a sign of pregnancy" (p. 357), in order to illustrate further how vermin in the unconscious often stand for babies, children, and thus for siblings. It is commonly observed that children (and later, adults) often use insects, fish, and even large animals as displaced objects to receive their unacceptable feelings and thoughts about—and less often their libidinal investments in—the siblings' representations.

In fact, psychoanalytic literature suggests that children and adults use animals, real or imaginary pets (Burlingham, 1952; Sherick, 1981), for expression of a wide range of unconscious processes. Insect, fish, birds, and animals that are not pets also stand for a variety of symbolic expressions. For example, a snake can stand for a phallus (Freud, 1900), a red fox for a menstruating woman (Volkan and Ast, 1994), and a spider for a smothering mother (Sperling, 1952). It should be emphasized that the symbols of a phallus, a menstruating woman, or a smothering mother will have incorporated the child's own personal projections onto them, making them unique to that person. A systematic study of the "mental zoo" in our psychic lives is presented by Akhtar and Volkan (in press).

Child psychoanalysts may observe children's developing attachment to animals in vivo, so to speak, while treating their young patients. Kupfermann (1977), for example, illustrates a variation in a child's use of animal symbols in a sibling-related trauma. Arthur, at the age of 2 1/2, was traumatized by the birth of twin brothers, but also by the dismissal of his beloved nursemaid. Searching for the comfort and closeness lacking in his relationship with his mother, he formed an intense and affectionate relationship with the family dog, whom he often imitated. His behavior indicated that he identified with the dog.

Insect, fish, bird, and animal symbolism abounds in the unconscious. In this book we specifically address how these symbols relate to the mental representations of siblings in adults, as illustrated by the following three adult cases of animal, fish, and bird symbolism.

CATS

A 38-year-old single woman began treatment with Dr. Eli Zaller because of a feeling of abandonment. She also complained of claustrophobia. From childhood on she had fears of being trapped in elevators and of flying in airplanes, and recently these fears had increased. She connected the beginning of her present mental condition to the death of her father five years earlier. At that time she was living with a boyfriend who was a couple of years younger. She became pregnant and had an abortion. The deaths of her father and her fetus, combined with the later rejection by the boyfriend, had increased her sense of abandonment and her fear of enclosed spaces.

Her name was Christine but she called herself Chris, as if she were a man. She spoke of her women friends and acquaintances in a degrading manner, saying that these women were interested only in their children and that they talked endlessly about them and of little else. Christine never wanted to get pregnant and have a child because she did not want the shape of her body to change. Instead of having children, she reported, she was devoted to her cats. She referred to children as "intruders" in one's life. In contrast, cats were not intruders. All of her adult life Christine had two cats. When she started her treatment she had two cats, one male and one female. She made reference to these animals in her first therapeutic session as if to introduce them to the therapist as her family members. Early in her treatment she would ask her therapist if they could cut short her sessions so that she could go home to feed her cats.

Christine was born into a Catholic family. Her father was a blue-collar worker and her mother had devoted herself to religion. Christine was the oldest child. Her brother was born three years later and her sister nine years later. Between the births of her two siblings her mother had a child who lived only one day. Since the family was rather poor when Christine was a child, she shared a bedroom with her brother and competed with him, especially for her father's love. She was extremely jealous when the father did "manly things" with his son. During her treatment it was learned that little Christine had identified with aspects of her brother and wanted to possess his penis and be a little boy herself. This was one of the reasons why in adulthood she dressed like a man and answered to a male name.

After her third offspring died Christine's mother became depressed. She got pregnant again, at age 41, eventually to give birth to Christine's sister. The baby girl was premature and needed a great deal of attention, especially from mother. Meanwhile the father kept doing "manly things" with Christine's brother. Christine felt abandoned.

The little sister, whom Christine in her sessions called an "an intruder," stayed in the parent's room for a few months and then began sharing Christine's bed. In fact, for about a year and a half Christine had to sleep in the same bed with her baby sister. She recalled that the mattress was too soft and that when she and the baby slept together they would roll into the middle of the bed. Her own territory literally was invaded. This would make her nights very difficult; the baby would cry and wake her up frequently. On the conscious level she called her baby sister "adorable and cute," but as we will see, her experience with her sister combined with her competition with her brother made Christine's sibling rivalry very strong: she actually resented her sister. Behind her reaction formation—describing the baby with kind words, for example—was her murderous rage toward both siblings and their mental representations. As an adult she wanted to control her relationship with these mental representations in order to control her murderous rage and the guilt that resulted from it. She had displaced her brother's mental representation into her boyfriends, who were always younger than she. Soon after she began treatment she and a man named Frederick became lovers. Frederick was eight years younger than Christine and she described him as a man-child and under her control. She would allow him to have intercourse with her only once a month. Frederick's place in her life was secondary to the cats' place in her life. Her cats roamed all over her house and slept in her bed. But whenever she wished she could kick them out of her bed or bedroom and lock them up elsewhere in the house. She needed to have a sense of control over the cats' actions and what territory they could occupy.

During her first year of treatment Christine began exhibiting behavior concerning her unconscious territorial fantasies about her mother's womb. For example, Dr. Zaller's waiting room symbolically evolved into a womb. Christine would spend hours speaking about who should control the door to the waiting room. The therapist habitually opened the waiting room door to invite his patient to her sessions. This frustrated Christine because she did not want anyone to "control" the door of the waiting room but herself. If she took charge of opening or closing the door she unconsciously would control what babies came in or out of the womb. During her first year in treatment, one day her therapist arrived two minutes late for her session. This incident evolved into a "therapeutic story" (Volkan, 1984). The patient, for the next few months, did not want to pay the therapist's full fee, but withheld *two* dollars to compensate for the lost two minutes.

Focusing on the "therapeutic story" it became clear that the number two held symbolic importance for Christine—it stood for her two siblings. The patient wanted to deprive the therapist of the two dollars, her two siblings. She wanted to be the sole child of the therapist.

Christine's understanding of the dynamics of her preoccupation with Dr. Zaller's waiting room and the story of the two dollars led her to realize the meaning of her *two* cats. The two cats represented her two siblings. She called the cats "adorable and cute"—the same adjectives she had used to describe her baby sister. Since her mother was allergic to cats, during her visits to Christine's house, the mother would not pay attention to the cats or take care of them. During such times Christine would become her mother's sole "child."

When her transference neurosis fully developed, the patient one day managed to come to Dr. Zaller's office complex early with a package of cheese and put it into the refrigerator next to the waiting room. The analysis of this event showed that the therapist's refrigerator (an enclosed space like an elevator or an airplane) was his symbolic womb and that Christine wanted to control its contents. The cheese, on one level, stood for the patient herself, but when it smelled and had to be "expelled" from the refrigerator, it stood for the siblings and her corresponding hateful self representation.

In the second year of her treatment, Frederick's married sister had twins. Christine and Frederick took an airplane to visit the mother with her two babies. Armed with what she had learned so far in the treatment Christine was able to observe her reactions to being in an enclosed space (the airplane) and to the twins. After she worked through the reactions to that trip the therapist began noticing changes in Christine. She no longer wanted to be called Chris, and instead demanded that her friends call her Christine. She began to visit adoption clinics in order to adopt a child. But, frequently, she made slips of the tongue and called adoption clinics *abortion* clinics, exhibiting her ambivalence about having children, and this ambivalence connected to her wish to get rid of (abort) her siblings.

She and Frederick moved to a larger house in the third year of her treatment. At this time the meaning of the cats began to change. They became the "wanted" children; Christine began exercising "good" mothering behavior toward them by taking care of the cats as if they were newborn children. Instead of controlling them she began learning how to love them. She also got some dental work done, bought feminine clothing, and began accepting her womanhood.

When she reached the age of 41 memories of her mother at age 41 having a baby (Christine's sister) began pouring out. After working through her conflicts about these memories, Christine became pregnant. Throughout her pregnancy she worked through more of her feelings about her siblings' representations. When she gave birth to a girl, Christine was surprised that the child was not damaged. Then, still in her treatment, the new mother developed an erotic oedipal transference. The resolution of it ultimately led to the termination of her treatment, at which time the patient was considering marrying Frederick.

When her treatment, which lasted six years, terminated, Christine's child was old enough to go to a daycare center, and Christine as a proud mother got involved in many activities there. During these times her preoccupation with cats disappeared—they were just pets! Then, just before her therapy terminated, the female cat ran away. Christine grieved over losing this cat. It is of course impossible for us to say for sure whether or not the cat had sensed that Christine had turned her attention to her baby, and that it left because owner's cathexis to her (the cat) no longer existed!

HORSES

Volkan (1987) describes the case of Pattie who was traumatized by the birth of a sister who had orthopedic difficulties with her legs. The mother's attention turned to her youngest daughter, leaving Pattie at the mercy of her oral aggression, which later condensed with anal and phallic sadism. Many years later, while working on a farm, she saw that two horses had badly injured their legs. Pattie followed the customary "cure" and shot them. She had no remorse over killing the two injured horses.

When Pattie's older sister had a baby, Pattie dreamed that she and her older sister were pulling a trailer containing a horse.

The trailer turned into a boat which Pattie and her sister took to a family reunion. When she left the older sister and the horse on the shore, Pattie's mother, who was present at the reunion, asked her, "Should we go back and get your sister and the horse?" Pattie replied "No! She can take care of herself!" The dream occurred after Pattie saw her sister for the first time with her new baby. Pattie, in spite of her expressed feelings of not wanting to be a mother, had recently become pregnant and terminated the pregnancy by abortion. Pattie's mother, during a visit with her daughter and grandchild, showered the baby with affection and did not ask how Pattie was feeling. The dream suggests that Pattie wished to turn her mother's attention to herself and to leave her sister and her baby behind. The horse represented the older sister's baby. While associating to this dream Pattie realized how the injured horses on the farm represented her younger sister who had a deformity in her legs. Her lack of remorse over killing the horses had come from her displacement of her sister's mental representation onto them. Only much later and after her conflictual relationship with the representations of her siblings was worked through in analysis, did Pattie experience sadness for killing the two horses.

While in analysis Pattie became a horse trainer. One day just prior to her entering the termination phase, she brought along a blood sample from a horse. Knowing that there was a refrigerator near the analyst's office, she stored the blood sample in it before coming to her appointment. She told Dr. Volkan what she had done and explained that after her session she had to take the blood sample to a veterinarian. She asked if she had been right to do this. The analyst gave his approval, but suggested that they might pursue the possible significance of her behavior. It turned out that Pattie wanted to demonstrate to the analyst that her drawing the blood from the horse was not dangerous for it, but actually for its benefit. She had wanted to show the analyst in a concrete way that she had tamed her aggression toward horses/siblings. During this session Pattie recalled shooting the two horses. She also commented that she was in a risky business (horse training), but that her increased professionalism, her increased understanding of and control over the aggression she projected onto the horses-siblings, had made her career less dangerous.

BIRDS

Bird symbolism pertaining to a sibling appears in Berman's (1978) analysis of a 46-year-old physician whose baby sister died when he was 3 years old. As an adult this man exhibited a profound unconscious sense of guilt, a repetitive need for self-punishment, and a negative therapeutic reaction in analysis.

The physician was very interested in and devoted to birds. He felt protective toward them and was outraged when he noticed others' cruelty toward birds. Since age 12 he had been an avid bird watcher. His conscious belief was that his devotion to birds had started when he was 4 or 5 years old; he thought that at that age he had shot a nesting dove with an arrow and killed the bird. He also had a memory of having discovered this bird's eggs in a nest. Berman does not tell us whether this memory was a screen memory. Nevertheless, the physician recalled in his analysis how he had become overcome with grief when he discovered the eggs, and since then he had felt that he "owed a debt to birds."

The physician also had birds as pets. He had had a parrot for fifteen years and he called this bird "my baby." During his analysis he made an association between his protective and tender attitude toward the birds and his becoming a physician and protecting his patients. But he was always worried that he might make an error and "kill" someone.

The analyst interpreted that at a deeper level the birds represented the patient's baby sister and that the physician unconsciously felt responsible for her death and believed he owed her a debt. The patient's initial response to this interpretation was disbelief that an incident so far back in his life could continue to affect him. However, he began to make associations that supported Dr. Berman's interpretation. He had never visited the baby's grave, but he was in the habit of praying for the departed soul of his sister. Soon after these sessions he began to have dreams of pregnancy and birth.

The patient had a hemangioma in the shape of a leaf. The family story was that this mark on his skin resulted from his mother's being frightened by a snake crawling out from under some leaves when she was pregnant with him. The patient had made a study of snakes in his locality and concluded that the snakes in this area were only harmful to infants and small children. Slowly, the patient's unconscious fantasy was reconstructed. He was born bearing the sign of the leaf—which equaled the snake. *He* was the snake who could kill infants and small children and eat and kill small birds (his infant sister).

FISH

The traumatic influence of a mother's pregnancy and a sibling's birth may not make itself conveniently available to an adult patient's conscious mind or to the analyst's observing eye. During treatment, though, an external event may trigger it to surface in a symbolic fashion. In the following vignette, a patient's dream about a fish and a cat illustrates how an external event reactivated childhood self and object representations and associated feelings about a sibling birth and transformed these into symbolic elements in her dream.

Janet, a woman in her early thirties, sought treatment for marital problems. She had married an older man who had a grown daughter from a previous marriage. During the end of the second year of Janet's analysis, the daughter came to live with them. The patient reported a favorable conscious reaction to this arrangement. Janet thought that the step-daughter, who was 11 years younger, would provide good company and that she would help to diffuse the persistent tension between Janet and her husband. In fact things did seem to work out well for a couple of months, until the analyst announced his upcoming three-week vacation. As the date for the absence approached, Janet decided to stop having sexual intercourse with her husband because of her angry feelings toward him. She could not identify the reason for her anger. Then, in one analytic session, Janet reported an "unusual happening." Not wishing to remain in her marital bed with her husband, and because the stepdaughter now occupied "her bed" (the bed in the guest room that Janet had slept in as a teenager), Janet went to the basement and without any form of bedding slept on the floor. In spite of the discomfort she fell asleep and had a dream: "I dreamt of a small fish swimming in a fish bowl. It was pink and it had a face like the face of a baby.

The baby-faced fish attempted to get out of the water, and put its head outside of the narrow rim of the bowl. At this time a mean-looking cat appeared and attacked the fish. I woke up anxious." Janet perceived her sleeping on the floor as a form of punishment, but she did not know why she wanted to punish herself. Her associations to the dream made her aware of guilt feelings pertaining to her emotional reactions to her mother's pregnancy and her only sibling's birth. The age difference between Janet and her sibling was 11 years—the same as between Janet and her stepdaughter. Physically mature at age 11, Janet had been approaching her pubertal years and had begun her "second individuation" process (Blos, 1979), a revisitation of the mental representations of her parents and other important persons in her childhood environment and a reexamination of ambivalence toward them, as well as reprocessing separation-individuation and oedipal issues.

Here we must provide some necessary background information. Janet was born in a European country to an American military man and his wife, a native of that country. When Janet was a child of oedipal age, her father was captured in a neighboring country during one of his spy missions. This was an important "object loss" in her life: the "loss" of an oedipal father combined with the "loss" of her mother's attention because of preoccupation with her husband's fate. Janet regressed and began to cling to her mother. Even though the father returned home after two years, the damage had been done—the mental representation of drastic "object losses" and its consequences had crystallized in Janet's mind.

The family moved to the United States a year before the birth of her sibling. Unable to speak fluent English and the product of a nationally mixed marriage, she felt different, and this alienation along with low self-esteem made Janet overly cautious. She remained dependent on her mother and developed a fearful attitude toward her new world. In time she might have adjusted to her new environment and more successfully navigated her adolescent passage had she not then experienced yet another object loss: her mother's pregnancy and the birth of a sibling. Feelings and reactions for losses pertaining to her father's capture and the move to a new country were condensed with the birth of a sibling.

The stepdaughter's "intrusion" into her territory coinciding with the analyst/mother's rejection (his approaching vacation), reawakened her reactions to her mother's pregnancy and the resulting birth. The stepdaughter occupied "her bed" just as her sibling had taken her place in her mother's attention. Janet's unconscious low self-esteem rendered her second-class citizen status—sleeping on the hard basement floor.

The baby-faced pink fish in a bowl in her dream represented her sibling in her mother's belly. The bowl with a narrow opening symbolized the mother's womb. The sibling was about to be born—attempting to get out of a body of water. Janet understood that she was the "mean" cat, her self representation infused with aggression toward her sister and the mother who inflicted a trauma on her. She "punished" herself for her aggression and slept on the basement floor which she likened to a floor in a jail.

Events from different stages of her life were linked. Circumstances of the present day clearly linked with events from when she was 11 and these connected with events from her childhood in Europe. There her feelings of "loneliness" caused by her father's capture had given rise to a relationship with an imaginary horse, but as an adult, she created a different imaginary playmate. She reported to her analyst that while lying on the basement floor, she had "created" a lover in her imagination, based on an actual man whom she knew but with whom she had never been intimate, who soothed her psychic wounds as had her imaginary horse in the past.

A closer look at this story reveals further elements of condensation. For example, by sleeping on the basement floor, Janet "remembered in action" the separation from her father. Until this time she could not recall the details of her father's capture or her reactions to it. One thing was clear, however: the family did not know for many months if he was alive and if he would return. At one point, the little girl learned that his captors had put him in jail. Her frame of reference about "jails" came from the television shows she had seen, and she imagined him lying on the floor of a prison cell. By identifying with her father "in jail," she partly denied having suffered that object loss.

She had repressed the influence of her mother's pregnancy and the birth of her sibling until now. The incident of "kicking myself out of my bed" and its analysis removed the repression. Now she saw clearly how the intrusion of the new baby in her adolescent life, condensed with earlier psychological events, played a role in her adult behavior patterns. For example, she feared having a child. She avoided motherhood, attempting by displacement to undo the fact that her mother had had a second child. Additionally, she understood that she covertly hated her stepdaughter, who represented her little sister. In her attempts to avoid motherhood she would become angry with her husband, fearing that their sexual encounters might lead to pregnancy. Her anger effectively blocked his sexual advances, and the frustration in the couple's sex life underlay their marital difficulty.

Besides the animal symbolism (in the form of a fish) in Janet's dream, we see evidence of territoriality and womb fantasies. These are the topics we study in the next chapter.

4 TERRITORIALITY AND UNCONSCIOUS WOMB FANTASIES

We have already alluded to territoriality and unconscious womb fantasies in the previous chapter. Here we examine these two phenomena in some detail and illustrate them with more clinical material. These phenomena clearly relate to a particular symptom: claustrophobia. Claustrophobia can appear in childhood and continue into adulthood. Sometimes this symptom does not exist in childhood but an event that reactivates the sibling experience of childhood in the adult's mind (e.g., the birth of one's baby, the death of one's mother) can lead to the development of claustrophobia in adulthood. Abarbanel (1983) illustrated, for example, that some women's sibling experiences are revived during their second pregnancies, as mother and firstborn await the new arrival. We know of two cases where men's unconscious sibling experiences awakened and then induced symptoms when their wives gave birth to second babies, which unconsciously reminded the husbands of the birth of their own siblings. One of the two is the case of Stewart, which we report in this chapter. In chapter 11 we refer to Harry, whose sibling's wife's giving birth to a child initiated psychopathology.

In a classic paper Lewin (1935) explained that claustrophobia and fear of suffocation in enclosed locations relate to unconscious fantasies of being in the mother's womb. Lewin referred
to the unconscious expectation of "meeting" one's father's penis
in the mother's womb, but he did not make reference to a fantasy of
siblings in the womb. Without directly mentioning claustrophobia,
Arlow (1969a) also describes how an enclosed space can symbolically stand for a womb, and unlike Lewin, he does make reference
to siblings. For example, he says that if a patient refers to being in a
bus, the therapist should be alerted to the possibility of the patient's
reactivating part of a fantasy concerning pregnancy or being within
a claustrum. One of Arlow's patients recalled a dream while she was
cleaning out a closet. Her dream concerned being in a diving bell
and having an encounter with a shark swimming outside of it (not
unlike Janet's dream in which a cat waits for a fish to come out of a
bowl). The shark attempted to devour the patient, who was one of
a set of identical twins. In general she was preoccupied with impulses of hostility and competition toward her sibling. The analysis
of this patient's dream illustrated that "emptying junk out of a
closet in reality was in fantasy killing a rival in a claustrum"
(p. 37).

Our own experience with patients who fear enclosed spaces
also suggests that the patient's symptoms often relate to unconscious fantasies concerning mental representations of younger
siblings and the mother's pregnancy with the younger siblings.
The child develops an unconscious fantasy that the inside of the
mother's belly should belong to her. The child wishes to enter it
and "kill" the new fetus. This causes a conflict: the wish to "kill"
the fetus clashes with a fear of losing mother—because she is the
carrier of the fetus—and her love or of being punished by the
superego. The conflict produces anxiety and the child develops
a phobia in the service of absorbing the anxiety. A phobia requires
two mental mechanisms to occur simultaneously: displacement
and avoidance. The child displaces her mother's womb onto an
enclosed space, such as a closet, and then fears and therefore
avoids being there.

There are variations on this theme. Sometimes the patient
projects her aggression onto the fetus and then fears to enter
into mother's womb (enclosed space) even while wishing to do

so, because if she enters the womb she will face a fetus made dangerous by her own projections. Before proceeding further we should mention that after a child struggles with oedipal issues she also may have fears due to an unconscious fantasy of the father's penis in the mother's womb. In some cases the representation of the father's penis and of a sibling in the mother's womb become condensed.

TERRITORIALITY

Claustrophobia involves territoriality. Scholars who study animal behavior tell us that to understand territoriality is a step toward understanding man's evolutionary nature. Ardrey (1973) writes:

> As important as territory to social animals—and we may find some-day that it is more important—is the compulsion to achieve status within one's society. Territoriality is essentially defensive, an in-ward mechanism aiding us to defend what we have; status is essen-tially aggressive, an inward pressure to achieve dominance over our social partners. In the arena the two innate forces combine to bring about a single pattern. Through the holding of territory, we defend what social status we have achieved; by challenging our neighbors, we attempt to better ourselves [p. 69].

Some birds and animals, such as crows, robins, wolves, and antelopes, unmistakably express territoriality. Humans have adapted to the environment (Hartmann, 1939) in such a way that territoriality similar to that shown openly by other social animals cannot easily be observed in humans. What is common in humans—especially among those who come to see us as patients having complicated relationships with the representations of their siblings—is the existence of unconscious fantasies of owning the territory of the mother's belly and having to defend it against intruders. One may argue that the potential for territoriality is biologically determined. The appearance of unconscious womb fantasies, as Kleinians would say, may derive from an inherited aspect of the aggressive drive. We feel comfortable, however, in falling back on our *restricted* way of describing unconscious fanta-sies (see chapter 1). As stated earlier we surmise that the child's unconscious territoriality and womb fantasies result from the child's "interpretation," in stressful situations, of wishes, fears, perceptions, and feelings pertaining to experiences with a pregnant mother and a new sibling. Since these experiences have certain common characteristics—for example seeing mother's swollen belly and mother's attention to what is in her belly—womb and territoriality fantasies are similar across cultures. For example, we have seen them occurring in the United States in individuals from different ethnic and racial backgrounds, and we have seen them in German and Turkish patients with whom we have worked psychoanalytically. Although the details in ethnic, cultural, economic, and familial backgrounds of the cases varied considerably, certain key symptoms matched.

ROBERT REDFORD'S HAND

In the following brief case report the patient did not seek analysis because of claustrophobia, but developed it as layers of other unconscious defenses against sibling experiences were stripped away during treatment. Stewart, a lawyer, came to analysis because of his masochistic attitude at the big law firm where he worked. He secretly competed with a younger colleague, but then sabotaged his own efforts for advancement. He kept saying, "If I win, the younger guy will be hurt. I can't hurt this guy." His analysis revealed that he had severe sibling rivalry and that the younger lawyer stood for his younger and only brother, born when the patient was 3 years old. The birth of his sibling had been traumatic for the patient. When his mother was pregnant with his brother, his father left for military duty, and the lawyer slept with his pregnant mother in her bed. When little Stewart reached oedipal age he "reprocessed" the memories of this event in the light of his new way of looking at things, creating elements of an oedipal triumph.

When his brother came along, little Stewart had to leave his mother's bed and room. Occupying a crib next to his mother's bed and replacing him in her bedroom, the new baby seemed also to have replaced him in his mother's attention. His mother felt depressed at that time and barely had enough energy to look after the new baby. The lawyer recalled hearing stories about how he suffered months of nightmares and crying spells as he demanded to be returned to his mother's bed, though he did not consciously remember those terrifying experiences himself.

During the middle period of his analysis the lawyer's wife gave birth to the couple's new son. They already had a 3-year-old boy, so the structure of his new family now matched that of his childhood family when his sibling arrived. Around the same time, one of Stewart's childhood (male) friends died in a car accident. These two incidents occurring so close together prompted the development of new symptoms in the lawyer. At first he became intensely afraid of dying in a car accident, and he took elaborate precautions while driving. Fear of being in a car then generalized to a fear of being in various enclosed spaces. Soon his claustrophobia was accompanied by obsessive thoughts about killing his 3-year-old son. He also became very anxious if his older son even touched the baby.

One day when he took his 3-year-old son to an amusement park they passed by a pond. He felt an urge to push his son into the water. In his imagination, however, he himself would dive into the water to save the boy, at the last minute, from drowning. During analysis he made the following series of associations to his thoughts at the amusement park.

The birth of his second son reactivated in his mind his experience with the birth of his brother. He felt abandoned and hostile toward the sibling for causing his abandonment; then, because he wanted to get rid of his sibling, he felt guilty. He did not want his older son to touch the baby lest he (the patient at the age of 3) kill the baby (the lawyer's own brother). He had displaced himself onto his 3-year-old son. At the amusement park, Stewart now recalled, he had first had a daydream of his 3-year-old son swimming in the pond and having fun. It was after this pleasurable daydream that he wanted to push his son into the water and "kill" him. He ended up "saving" the boy in his conscious fantasy. It should be recalled that his visit to the amusement park had taken place after Stewart's friend's death, which had made the idea of death painfully real for him.

The analysis of his daydreams revealed the following: it was Stewart, as a 3-year-old child, who wanted to swim—in his mother's belly. He would take charge of "his" territory and not allow his brother to enter it. He felt guilty and the pleasurable feelings gave way to his directing aggression toward his son, who represented himself as a murderous youngster. Thus this original daydream was replaced by his impulse to push his son into the pond and "kill" him. In the long run his sense of self-preservation made him have another daydream so that he could save his drowning son. We also suspect that at this point of his experience at the park, when he thought of killing him, his son also represented his brother and his newborn child.

After Stewart understood the above unconscious underpinnings of his daydreams, he began to have a nightly recurring dream about a closet (an enclosed space) that made him feel anxious. The closet, placed outdoors, was covered with vines. He would push apart the vines and find a lock on the wooden door. Although quite curious about the contents of the closet, the anxious feelings it induced in him made him run away from the place. He said, "I am phobic about this closet." The analyst sensed that the closet represented the lawyer's mother's womb and the vines her pubic hair. He said nothing, however, but awaited the evolution of the therapeutic process. Meanwhile, the patient unrepressed more memories about his childhood and his sibling experiences and this led to his further understanding of the influence of his childhood experiences on him.

One day as soon as he lay down on the analytic couch Stewart declared, "I know what is in the closet. Last night I had my closet dream again, but this time I collected my courage and opened the lock and the closet door. It was dark and moist inside. The floor had water that looked like the water at the pond at the amusement park. I slowly entered the closet. There was something in the water and in spite of my heart's pounding I picked it up; it looked like a fetus—like those I have seen pictures of. When I lifted it up it suddenly changed; it turned into a hand and grabbed my hand which was holding it. I felt very scared and woke up. I knew, however, that the hand in the dream belonged to Robert Redford."

The night before he had this dream the patient had gone to see a movie directed by Robert Redford entitled, *A River Runs Through It.* The movie's theme centers around the relationship between two brothers and the death of the younger one. Stewart's associations to Robert Redford (Stewart's younger brother's nickname is "Red" because of the color of his hair and Red drives a *red Ford*) helped him to understand that his claustrophobia was due to his aggression toward his brother, and by extension, toward his newborn son. He feared entering enclosed spaces because he did not want to face a dangerous brother, a mental representation saturated with Stewart's own projected aggression. In the dream he met the dreaded object, "red Ford," initiating an intensive working through of his internalized relationship with the representation of his sibling. Following the analysis of this dream and further work on his territoriality and womb fantasies Stewart's claustrophobia disappeared. Eventually, the initial symptoms of his obsessive and masochistic relationship with the younger colleague at work, which had brought him to analysis, also resolved.

A CHILD WHO HID IN A MAILBOX

Evidence of unconscious fantasies pertaining to the mother's womb and intrusion into one's territory by a younger sibling comes from clinical observations in the case of Stewart. These kinds of unconscious fantasies do not always cause claustrophobia; sometimes they are expressed with other symptoms or behavior patterns, including counterphobic activities such as ritually entering enclosed spaces and thus reenacting the fantasy. Now we present the case of Hamilton, who had claustrophobic behavior as an adult, but who, as a child, exhibited ritualistic behavior about being in an enclosed tight space. The childhood behavior eventually converted to a phobia in adulthood.

The details of Hamilton's case, focusing on his personality disorder, have been written and published by us elsewhere (Volkan and Ast, 1992). Here we focus on only the material relevant to our topic. Hamilton, a businessman, was in his late fifties when he became Dr. Volkan's analysand. Initially, he suffered from depressive feelings initiated by his second (and much younger) wife's rejection of him. His first wife had died many years earlier.

Hamilton's claustrophobia was hidden beneath many other symptoms. But it revealed itself in his fear of being alone in his bedroom. To offset his phobia he always planned to have a woman with him at night. This woman always had to be a "good" woman. Hamilton usually could not sleep with the same woman two nights

in a row, feeling that on the second night the woman might turn
into a "bitch." Therefore he had many girl friends and alternated
sleeping with them. As long as he had a "good" woman with him
he experienced no fear of being alone in his bedroom. When
rejected by women and feeling alone, Hamilton also feared entering his parked car at night, thinking that somebody could have
hidden in the car and would attack him.

Hamilton was the third child in his family. Eighteen months
after his birth a baby sister arrived, followed by another after a
similar interval. Thus by the age of 3 Hamilton had had to deal
with his mother's two pregnancies and the arrivals of two siblings.
In his analysis we learned that his mother had suffered from postpartum depression after delivering each of her last two children.
These siblings' births were not "average, expectable events"
(Parens, 1980) for little Hamilton.

A black girl named Abigail, probably in her late teens, was
hired at the time and assigned to take care of Hamilton. Abigail's
presence seems to have compensated for his mother's preoccupation with his younger siblings and her postpartum depression.
But Abigail one day "disappeared" from his life. He was then 4
years old. The explanation seems to have been that Hamilton's
parents discovered that Abigail was pregnant, and they dismissed
her at once. The child had no preparation for this loss.

Hamilton's family moved to a farm soon after Abigail's dismissal. So, besides losing his mother to her depression and his
siblings and experiencing abandonment by Abigail, Hamilton's
surroundings also had changed. His screen memory of his early
life at this farm concerned his looking out from a window and
seeing a frozen and empty field. Screen memories are compro-
mises between allowing the recollection of a painful experience
and denying its existence, the person involved recalling something less painful than the actual experience but still associated
with some of its affects. The analysis of a screen memory often
reveals a more fearful experience. Hamilton's case analysis revealed that he had felt deserted as a child and had experienced
a childhood depression. He had a second screen memory which
referred to his attempt to deny his childhood depression. The
second memory concerned seeing his mother's beautiful breasts
while she bathed (she was then in her early thirties). As an adult

Hamilton almost nightly slept with "good" women who were in their early thirties. He would compare their breasts with his childhood "vision" of his mother's breasts. Sometimes he would sleep with "good" women who had darker skins or black hair. They represented the "good" Abigail. Without satisfying his "addiction" to these "good" women he would experience anxiety, because he would be once more overwhelmed by the affects connected with his childhood abandonments. Without the presence of a "good" woman, his bedroom (the womb) would be dangerous because of Hamilton's unconscious aggression toward the "bad" mother who had abandoned him. We will study Hamilton's experiences with his younger siblings and how these experiences "settled in" his adult mind by keeping a focus on his childhood history as briefly described above.

The birth of his siblings were associated with his childhood losses. In real life, as an adult, he exhibited conscious and often extreme sibling rivalry toward his siblings and even toward his own children. Attending the birthdays of his children and grandchildren would induce anxiety in him. At such times he would often look frantically for new "good" women with whom to have sex. The critical thing was not the sex itself, but his entering into a "good" woman. He placed no importance upon who the partner was: all "good" women were interchangeable in his mind. They represented the wished-for loving mother into whose body he would enter. Early in his analysis, separation from his analyst on *Labor Day* was hard for him since the word *labor* recalled the delivery of a child. Thus the analyst's unavailability on Labor Day symbolically represented the absence of the analyst/mother to bear a child.

The births of his younger siblings were traumatic for Hamilton. He was conscious of this as well as that some of his behavior reflected his reaction to these traumatic events. The reconstruction of his unconscious womb fantasy—his wish to be the only child in his mother's belly and to "kill" the intruders—however, could only be accomplished during his analysis. As a response to a brief separation from his analyst Hamilton recalled a large mailbox that stood about a mile from the family's farmhouse by a country road. Little Hamilton, just over 4 years old, would walk to the road with his two older siblings who had to wait near the mailbox for a horse-drawn carriage to take them to school. A motherly schoolteacher also waited for the carriage there, and little Hamilton noted that she usually sat on the mailbox while waiting. Deciding that his small body would fit into the box, Hamilton began a ritual of arriving at the road before the others came, sneaking into the box, shutting the lid, and making no sound to alert the teacher—a substitute for his mother—to his presence. After the carriage picked up its passengers he would climb out and go home. It should be recalled that at this time his depressed mother was preoccupied with his younger siblings and Abigail was gone; in addition his father was busy trying to run a farm during the Depression.

The meaning of this particular ritual, of a little boy hiding in an enclosed space, emerged when, in his transference reaction to his analyst, Hamilton began perceiving the analyst's office as the mailbox and the analyst as the motherly teacher. Returning to his mailbox story he amplified his recollections; he had felt as though he were in the teacher's belly while he sat in the box, which was draped in her skirts as she sat on it. In one dream associated with this memory he was an egg from which he emerged like a baby chicken. In his unconscious fantasy he was the sole occupant of his most prized territory: his mother's belly. In his childhood ritual (symptom) which had evolved as a reaction to his siblings' births, instead of claustrophobia we see its opposite: taking sanctuary in an enclosed space and by being its sole occupant "killing" his younger siblings.

When Hamilton became a teenager his internalized sibling experience exhibited itself in a different symptom. In this one his wish to "kill" the younger siblings was clearer. At the age of 14 Hamilton began visiting his youngest sister at night in her bedroom. He would rub his erect penis against her leg and ejaculate on it and then send her to the bathroom to wash, while he returned to his room. This incestuous ritual eventually made him feel so guilty that he stopped it.

Briefly, the incestuous behavior was mainly in the service of getting rid of his sister(s). In his fantasy he would make his sister pregnant and then his parents would send her away from their home just as they had fired Abigail for her pregnancy. His semen was associated in his mind with bullets coming out of his penis.

As an adult, then, his early sibling experience had condensed in his nightly ritual with "good" women: without the "good" women he was claustrophobic, but by entering into their bodies, as he had entered the mailbox of his childhood, he was "counterphobic." However, after he entered into a "good" woman's body and symbolically made her "pregnant," he avoided being with her the next night since now she had become "bad."

5 THE SECRET RESTAURANT

In the previous chapters we presented brief clinical vignettes to illustrate specific aspects of sibling experiences and adults' internalized interactions or identifications with the representations of siblings. We also focused on unconscious womb fantasies pertaining to pregnant mothers and the representations of younger siblings. In order to provide further and more convincing clinical proof of the existence of such unconscious fantasies, in this chapter we focus in some detail on the case of a young college student named Lisa, providing material from a one-year period of her analysis. It was during this time that her case clearly illustrated *all* of the concepts regarding younger siblings that we examined in the previous chapters: new sibling represented as intruder, animal symbolism, Christmas "neurosis," territoriality, murderous rage, unconscious womb fantasies, and claustrophobia. Lisa's case also demonstrates the centrality of analyzing unconscious sibling experiences during the treatments of certain patients. Without learning how Lisa's sibling experiences had "settled in" her adult mind, without recognizing the nature of her unconscious fantasies, and without resolving her transference neurosis and the conflicts associated with these fantasies, the analysis of her oedipal and other psychosexual and developmental issues would have been impossible.

LISA'S BACKGROUND

Lisa was referred to Dr. Volkan by a psychoanalytic colleague who had treated her for three months and thought that she suffered from a schizophrenic disorder, making her unsuitable for analysis "on the couch." He made the referral because he knew of Dr. Volkan's interest in difficult and regressed patients. Dr. Volkan's diagnostic interviews with Lisa indicated that she had a "psychotic core" (Volkan, 1995; Volkan and Akhtar, 1996) in which self and object representations were not clearly differentiated. This core was "enveloped" (H.A. Rosenfeld, 1965; D. Rosenfeld, 1992; Volkan, 1995) by a differentiated psychic structure. Lisa also had more anxiety than that usually associated with neurotic individuals. In a typical neurotic patient, anxiety serves as a signal pointing to internal dangers that the patient cannot fully understand or describe; instead the patient presents a rationalized cause for the anxiety. For Lisa, however, the anxiety was paralyzing. She would stop in the middle of a sentence—frozen and almost catatonic—unable to complete her sentence. Needless to say, obtaining a life story from Lisa proved difficult, but slowly her story emerged.

Lisa was the oldest child of a couple who had married quite young and had an immature relationship. While intelligent, they were unprepared for most of the duties of effective parenting. The unhappy marriage endured for twelve years. When Lisa was 2 years old, her brother Joe was born. After his birth her mother had to stay in the hospital for several months, due to medical complications. A maid cared for Lisa and her maternal grandmother cared for her infant brother, at their home. Their father essentially deserted the family for three or four months but he eventually returned.

Two years later, another brother, Mark, arrived, and following his birth Lisa's mother had pneumonia. Once again Lisa was traumatized by a sibling birth coinciding with another separation from her mother. The father took his two oldest children away "to give their mother a rest" for several months. While Lisa did not recall, on the conscious level, what "being away" from her mother was like, she did hear stories concerning the inadequacy of her father's care for her and her brother. They stayed on a farm in primitive conditions, while her father, trying to write a book during this time, did not concern himself with his children's welfare except to see that they were fed. Upon reuniting the family, the parents hired a woman to care for the children. Lisa recalls her as unloving toward her and as having an ugly-looking blind eye. The memory of the injured eye became a symbol of this woman's inadequate caretaking and Lisa's negative feelings for her and for her own mother.

Her parents were faculty members of a college, and they liked to engage in intellectual discussions with their colleagues. They encouraged Lisa's intellectuality, and her success in using her intellect masked her unsatisfied overdependency on her mother during her developmental years. Because of Lisa's beauty, she easily captured people's notice and she quickly learned that her smile could get her the attention she craved, even though that attention usually proved short-lived.

One day, which happened to be Lisa's twelfth birthday, her father helped the family move into a new house. During the day he moved some furniture and repaired a few things. Then, without warning, he said "good-bye" and left the family at the new house. This trauma, coming as it did during her adolescence, robbed Lisa of any chance to rework her fragile core self-concept through her "second individuation" (Blos, 1979). In fact, after her adolescent passage she crystallized an obsessional personality supported with extreme intellectualization, rationalization, and isolation mechanisms. Her crystallized personality further enveloped her fragile core. As a teenager she seemed like a "good girl"—beautiful, smart, and helpful to her mother and brothers at home. She seldom saw her father.

After high school she attended the university where Dr. Volkan works. Away from her home environment for the first time, she became even more dependent on her intellectual ability and her obsessionalism and became a "superstudent." She began a sexual relationship with a young man two years younger than she whom she "loved to *death*." As long as Jim was around she remained a "superstudent," who had adjusted to university life, or so it seemed; except that she had a fear of enclosed spaces, such as elevators and airplanes, a symptom she had contended with during most of her life.

Lisa's apparent stability changed when Jim left for the summer to work at a hotel on a Caribbean island. She became extremely anxious and almost psychotic. Jim sent Lisa a picture of himself emerging from the water. In the picture Jim looked like a fish surrounded by the rim of a bay in the background. Jim had written on the back that he enjoyed working on the island and that he would not be returning soon. She became preoccupied with thoughts of Jim, and "knew" that he would not return to her. Her claustrophobia increased and she felt paralyzed. Her studies suffered—she could neither finish reading sentences nor finish her spoken sentences. As the analyst later learned, her inability to complete sentences symbolically represented feeling "cut off" from others—right now from Jim.

INITIAL SYMPTOMS AND INTERPRETATIONS

Because of Lisa's inability to complete sentences during the beginning of her analysis, the analyst did not yet know her full life story. He noted certain oedipal themes, but sensed that these issues might be serving as a defense, a "reaching up" (Boyer 1971, 1983; Volkan 1976, 1995) the developmental ladder to cover up earlier intrapsychic problems. The analyst decided that Lisa needed psychoanalysis in order to modify her "enveloped" psychotic core and alter its influence. Having experience in the analysis of severely regressed patients on the couch, he began treating Lisa on the couch four times a week.

As Lisa's psychoanalysis began, the analyst experienced an unusual and unexplainable reaction to Lisa's paralyzed speech, her half-completed sentences. Instead of giving them his full attention, he began to feel sleepy and could hardly wait for the sessions to end. After this went on for a month or so, he consulted a psychoanalytic colleague regarding his peculiar response to his sessions with Lisa, but neither of them could come up with a satisfactory answer. The analyst decided to await further developments. When not drowsy, he felt most curious about his peculiar response. In the end, this response lasted for nine months; no other patient had induced so lasting a reaction in him.

At the end of this period, Lisa described her analytic experience as similar to an extremely anxious airplane ride. (In actuality, due to her fear of airplanes, she had flown just twice in her life.) She described the imaginary flight as riding in a plane that flew through puffy, often pink, clouds. After nine months of analysis she could finally see the land from the plane; this coincided with feeling more organized and able to complete sentences. At the same time, the analyst was able to remain more alert throughout the sessions.

Now that Lisa could communicate more effectively and the analyst listen more attentively, the latter learned a great deal about Jim and what he represented. Lisa referred to Jim as a "stuffed puppet." The analyst began to think that she had externalized the representations of her siblings into her lover, who was younger than she, "stuffing" him with the representations of her siblings. She also referred to Jim as a "bird." Her associations to the "bird" made her recall keeping a journal as a teenager. In the journal she had written that she felt like a bird with a cloth over it. The bird could only move its wings under the cover; it could not fly, and it felt suffocated. She linked this feeling to the anxiety of claustrophobia. Lisa stated that Jim "became" a bird after she saw the picture of him coming out of the "body of water." The analyst sensed that the bird stood for a baby in the womb (body of water), and he wondered to himself whether the bird represented a child in her mother's belly, but he refrained from verbalizing his understanding prematurely.

Lisa began bringing many dreams to her sessions; in them birds emerged from water, and other creatures underwent transformations (as does a fetus). In other dreams Lisa cut up the swollen bellies of various animals to examine their insides. Speaking of these dreams, one day she identified herself with her pregnant mother and sensed that she wanted to damage her (mother's) insides. Crying, she said she felt "weird" as if "there is an alive feeling in me." She felt as though she were bleeding internally, and the blood had filled up her body to her eyes. Slowly the analyst began interpreting the possibility of her having unconscious fantasies that stemmed from her perceptions and feelings about her mother's pregnancy and the births of her siblings, which had been very traumatic for her. The analyst told Lisa that as a child she might have wished that her mother had not been pregnant with her siblings or that her siblings had never been born. Lisa also was told that Jim, at one level, represented her siblings, and as long as she knew his whereabouts she felt all right. When Jim left her she could not "control" her relationship with her "brothers." Jim's picture showing himself emerging from a body of water symbolically represented for her the birth of a baby, and this had disturbed her.

The analyst, with some considerable relief, began to understand his own drowsiness during the initial *nine months* (gestation period) of Lisa's analysis: he had regressed "in the service of the other [the patient]" (Olinick, 1980, p. 7), and had allowed himself, unconsciously, to act as a reservoir of Lisa's externalized sibling representations. He had become a "suffocated bird" himself during Lisa's sessions, sometimes twitching or moving his arms, like the wings of a bird under a cloth, in order to stay awake or "alive." Lisa had been "killing" her sibling representations, located in the analyst! Meanwhile, those first nine months of analytic sessions also held another meaning. During this time Lisa experienced herself in a womb (a fantasized airplane flying in pink clouds), fearing suffocation. After nine months she had a "rebirth." She was "reborn" as the only baby of the analyst/mother.

EXCERPTS FROM A YEAR-LONG PERIOD OF LISA'S FURTHER ANALYSIS

Since it is beyond the scope of this book to report on Lisa's entire case, we have chosen a specific period, from one Christmas to the next, during which time we saw clear clinical evidence of her unconscious fantasies regarding her siblings' representations and related issues. This period begins two-and-one-half years after the beginning of Lisa's treatment. By this time her analytic work had enabled Lisa to have some understanding of her sibling experiences. Her understanding could be summarized as follows:

Lisa harbored murderous feelings toward her brothers because they "caused" her traumatic separations from her mother. She had embodied her negative feelings for them in her relationship with Jim. She felt subordinate to Jim, and yet she also felt the need to have absolute control over their relationship. As long as she could successfully love him "to death," she also controlled

her unconscious aggression toward him (her brothers). Her phobias about elevators and airplanes represented her wish to be in
her mother's belly, but her own aggression made her fearful,
because if she destroyed her mother's womb, even though she
would thus make it unavailable to her brothers, she would ultimately destroy her mother and herself. (She was also afraid of
facing her brothers, made dangerous by her projection of her
own aggression onto them.) These contradictory expectations
paralyzed her whenever circumstances, such as Jim's absence,
made her feel unable to control her unconscious sibling experiences.

Now we present, in sequential order, the therapeutic stories
of Lisa's sessions from a period spanning one Christmas to the
next. As one might expect, the themes of these therapeutic stories
are repetitious. Our patients repeat therapeutic stories in the service of working through their problems. It should be noted that
working through her unconscious fantasies was only possible after
Lisa's therapeutic stories more clearly became a part of her transference neurosis.

We begin our journey at the Christmas time two-and-one-
half years after Lisa came to see the analyst. We have divided
this year period roughly into months and have reported relevant
material from each month. By this means we hope that the reader
will easily follow the therapeutic developments and the emergence of transference stories concerning Lisa's womb fantasies
and her sibling representations.

January

Following a separation for the Christmas holidays, Lisa returned
to her sessions and reported that her mother and siblings had
visited her on Christmas Day. After their departure, she began
having fantasies that "intruders" (her word) might enter the
apartment she shared with two other female students. Even
though she took elaborate precautions to prevent this, such as
using several locks to lock the door to her bedroom and closing
every window at night, she still felt terrified. Eventually the analyst

told her that as they had approached the Christmas holidays, she had seemed to perceive Dr. Volkan as her mother going away to have a baby. After all, this was the time of celebrating the birth of a baby, Jesus. The analyst also told Lisa that seeing her mother with her brothers might have rekindled the feeling that they had "intruded" upon "her" space (mother's womb). He explained that she had equated her room with a symbolic womb into which she would not permit her brothers to enter. This was why Lisa used so many locks to shut herself into her bedroom. In spite of her precautions she felt terrified of "intruders," the representations of her siblings.

Soon after this interchange between the analyst and Lisa, she reported a dream in which she was alone in a dark room. The door, which swung in two halves, had a lock, but she feared someone entering anyway. The dream's day residue came from her having heard a door in her apartment open during the night. The boyfriend of one of her housemates had arrived to visit his girl friend. Lisa felt uncomfortable about "intruding" on their privacy by hearing this, but at the same time, she felt they had "intruded" upon her. Her associations to the dream related to the primal scene. In her mind the intrusion of the father's penis into the mother's womb condensed with the intrusion of her brothers into the same space.

The couple in question in the apartment were on the point of separation; the young man was going away, "abandoning" his lover. Their situation reminded Lisa of Jim abandoning her for the summer—the abandonment that initiated her seeking analysis. Although Jim had returned to her, their relationship had changed because of Lisa's newly acquired knowledge that at one level Jim stood for her brothers: she was now conscious of the way in which he was a "stuffed puppet." During this time she and Jim spoke often of stopping their love affair and going their separate ways, but they kept on together.

The analyst told Lisa that the room in the dream might represent a womb, and the door with two halves, her mother's genitalia. The intruders outside might be the brothers; she did not want her mother to be pregnant with them or to give birth to them since circumstances each time had led to her feeling abandoned. She responded to this explanation by recalling some childhood memories of her aggression toward her siblings, such as hitting one brother on the head with an ashtray.

During the next session Lisa reported a detailed *conscious* fantasy of herself and the analyst in a house together facing "intruders" from the outside. The intruders were her next younger brother Joe and her father "merged almost in one." Lisa felt that together with the analyst she could face them, since he (the analyst) was "strong."

The dream she had that night reflected this fantasy. In her dream she saw John Anderson, the presidential candidate, meeting with her family under a glass shelter. Since it was night, the shelter should have been lighted, but it was not. The glass shelter had vents in it. This period of Lisa's analysis took place during a United States presidential campaign. John Anderson's candidacy earned Lisa's support because he opposed the National Rifle Association. She noted that he had the same distinctive white hair as the analyst had. The analyst told Lisa that because Anderson opposed aggression, her dream indicated her wish, as it appeared in her conscious fantasy, that the analyst (with white hair) would "disarm" the "intruders".

Her wish to "kill" her brothers came out in her association with the missing lights. Her boyfriend Jim had no light on his bicycle, and on the evening before the dream she had thought of buying him one "to protect him from getting killed when he rode his bike at night" (reaction formation). She thought of doing this "good deed" without telling him first, but then she abandoned the idea because he would rebel at being "babied." The analyst explained that the lack of light in her dream acted as a kind of wish that Jim (representing her brothers, when they were babies) would be killed without lights, and thus unable to occupy the glass shelter (mother's womb). The vents in the shelter had multiple but related meanings. In addition to allowing her to "vent" her anger; they also provided a safety valve to avert an explosion of the accumulated anger within the womb.

February

Lisa had a dream about being in a house. That evening she had gone to bed feeling anxious from imagining that an armed person

was outside her apartment. The house in the dream was covered
with vines, which her brother Joe tried to climb, but he fell and
smashed his head. After reporting this dream Lisa spoke of a
time when Joe had hurt himself climbing trees, and suddenly she
realized that she had wanted him to get hurt. This led to discussing her "perverted feelings," her contemplation of doing
nasty or sadistic things to the children who played near her apartment. She became very anxious as the hour progressed, and
talked about feeling very guilty because of "all these plans to do
nasty things to children." She had a sudden thought about dying
in a car wreck, and she realized how this represented her fear
that those she might harm would retaliate or that her guilt might
hurt her. She associated the vines in the dream with pubic hair;
she did not want Joe to climb up, or into, their mother's womb.
She then mentioned that in the dream after Joe smashed his head
she had put it back together (undoing).

She also associated the vines to a spider web, which brought
up a vague memory of seeing Mark, her second brother, in a
room with their mother. Lisa fantasized that she was a spider in
a web on the ceiling looking down on baby Mark, who was like a
"bug," and who "bugged" her. Lisa then uncovered a childhood
daydream about killing her brothers by *eating* them. She was a
spider and her brothers were the bugs! In the middle of her
sessions around this theme, Lisa called to cancel a session because
of a *sore throat*. The analyst suspected that her condition related
to her cannibalistic fantasy. When she came in a few days later,
she stated that her *birthday* had fallen between the canceled session and the present one, and that her boyfriend had ignored it.
On her birthday she had had a sore throat and a fever, and she
fantasized that her illness came as a punishment for her cannibalistic impulses toward her brothers. While sick in bed she tried to
"mesmerize" herself into feeling peaceful by imagining herself
as "unborn" in her "mother's womb."

Since her aggressive impulses toward the representations of
her brothers were projected onto Jim during this month, Lisa's
desire to end her relationship with Jim increased. She asked the
analyst what to do; the analyst made no response. She cried and
stated that Jim had never realized how she had used him as a
"stuffed puppet" representing her brothers. "Maybe staying with

Jim kept me from having my real feelings about my brothers come to the surface," she said. As it turned out, she did not end her relationship with Jim at this time—she felt she had to stay with him in order to "control" him.

After having gone to a restaurant with her visiting mother and brother Mark, Lisa had a dream about two cats in a piano. The piano was a day residue: at the restaurant where they had gone that day, Lisa had impulsively struck a key on a piano as they walked by it to their table, and Mark *following* her, had done the same. In the dream, the piano had an opening which Lisa leaned against to keep the cats from entering. But they disappeared and she feared they were in the piano. She wondered if they could survive in there. Lisa said that the two cats represented her brothers. One was small and "acted like Mark had when he was little." Lisa's mother actually played the piano, and Lisa felt that the piano represented her mother's womb. After having interpreted this dream herself, Lisa talked about having read a book on wolves, which asserted that wolves would tolerate the presence of other wolves as long as the latter respected their territorial boundaries. This made her think that if she respected the boundaries between her and her brothers, they would not harm her and she would not harm them, and so she felt that the danger they represented would lessen.

Her wish to have boundaries between her territory and that of her brothers' representations, however, could not yet become a reality. When she went to a shopping mall where she saw "tons of babies and mothers," this made her feel "absolutely sick." On the couch she said, "I hate it. I know where these feelings come from but still it is icky." Soon after this, as she drove to her appointment with the analyst, she thought that she might kill somebody during her lifetime, but that she could not kill a stranger. The thought occurred to her that the analyst was *not* a stranger. Therefore, she could kill the analyst, who at that moment represented her siblings. The analyst reminded her about the first nine months of their work when she had "killed" him while she rode in an airplane in pink clouds (mother's womb).

The material we have presented thus far indicates that much analytic work was accomplished in February regarding Lisa's fantasies about her mother's womb and her sibling representations.

In the following dream, also reported during this month, Lisa began to understand her condensation of her sibling representations with the representations of her father's penis in her mother's womb. This dream involved a house standing on an oval-shaped property. Her associations indicated that this oval shape represented the shape of a womb. In the house there were babies. "As if I wanted to look into a womb and see my brothers, such a weird thing!" she said. One baby in the house in the dream had an unusually large head, and his eyes made a single Cyclops eye on top of his head. The analyst made the interpretation that this infant might represent her father's penis, an intruder, like her brothers, into the space she wanted for herself, and Lisa agreed.

March

In early March, Lisa reenacted her wish to look into her mother's womb. Through the help of a medical student friend, Lisa visited a place in the local medical center where they stored bottles containing the preserved remains of newborn infants who had died during or just after birth. She also looked at books with pictures of fetuses. She had made the visit without having told her analyst about it first. During the session following her visit to the medical center, she spoke of the strange impulse which had compelled her to do this. On the couch, she cried out, "Why am I so into this?" Then she added, "Wild! Wild! Like I want to look into a womb. It's bloody." She unrepressed a childhood memory. She sat before a table playing with her food as she ate it. This memory was interposed with the picture of open-heart surgery on a television screen, showing a hand reaching for and holding a human heart. It was "gushy and bloody! All this meat!"

At this point the analyst offered that one way a child might fantasize getting rid of her brothers would be to eat them. He reminded her of her childhood daydream of being a spider and eating bugs. She cried, "It's better than cutting them into pieces, taking them out of the womb, and letting their bodies rot in the ground!" She expressed surprise at her own response, calling it "very weird," but then she disclosed that she had "a phobia" about eating red meat, and never did. Eating it would make her "feel gross," she said, and she limited her consumption of flesh to chicken and fish. The analyst explained how her cannibalistic fantasies played a role in this particular symptom, and she responded, "I swear, I cannot believe what I am learning, but now, right now, I feel so upset."

She went on to say that there was another way to get rid of her brothers—she could burn them. Then she recalled that in their old hometown she had had a "fire phobia" for some time. She added that besides fearing an intruder, she also feared the possibility of fire wherever she lived. She did not ride the elevator to the analyst's office for fear of fires, she said. The analyst again interpreted that the elevator represented *his* womb. (Much later in Lisa's analysis, after working through her unconscious sibling experiences, she had to work through psychosexual issues concerning elevator symbols.)

April

Early in this month what she called her "stage play" with Jim began to come to an end. The analyst thought that she was pushing Jim away from her and thus he found a new girl friend. Lisa did not recognize this development until one weekend she caught Jim in his apartment with his new girl, and although Lisa went into a rage, she felt some relief. Instead of experiencing panic in the face of abandonment as she had done before, she now felt a range of feelings from anger to sadness.

With the possibility of ending her "stage play" outside of her analytic sessions, the analyst expected an intensification of her transference neurosis, since she now might use the analyst (instead of Jim) as her primary "stuffed puppet." Such a transference neurosis indeed developed. But it took some months for the analyst to fully notice it.

May Through Summer Months

A final separation from Jim did not occur overnight. It took vacillation, pain, and several months for the separation to finalize. The analyst did not interfere. While Lisa brought dreams, daydreams, and many associations to her sessions, in actuality the

analyst sensed that not much work on her transference neurosis
was accomplished during this period. Lisa was busy grieving. Furthermore, early in the summer she graduated from the university
and had to deal with real world issues. In order to continue with
her analysis she got a job as a waitress in a newly opened restaurant. When she informed the analyst about this development he
had no idea of the significance of the particular restaurant she
had chosen. In July, Lisa began dating David, and in August she
began to live with him.

First Two Months of Fall

In the beginning of Fall, the analyst noticed an uneasiness and
realized that Lisa was keeping him in the dark about her day-to-
day life. He knew little about David, the new house they shared,
her new friends, or the restaurant where she worked. It was as
though Lisa had her own territory which she would prevent the
analyst from either entering or knowing about.

In October the analyst began to feel drowsy again during his
sessions with Lisa. This time, of course, he remembered having
a similar reaction to Lisa's sessions during the first nine months
of her analysis. The analyst thought: She's killing me again. I am
once more the "stuffed puppet." He formulated in his mind that
Lisa had made the city her mother's womb and that she not only
was keeping the analyst away from this territory, she was also
"killing" him. With this understanding the analyst's drowsiness
disappeared.

November

In mid-November the analyst, who is also a university professor,
scheduled a lecture at the Student Union in one of the campus
buildings. Students had spread posters announcing his lecture
throughout the university. Seeing the posters had made Lisa anxious, and she arrived at one of her sessions rather agitated. The
analyst realized that Lisa had reversed her dominant transference
manifestation. Now the lecture hall had become the analyst's
womb, and *she* the intruder—because of her wish to go there

to see and hear him. Her anxiety indicated that she expected retaliation from him.

Through examining her anxiety, the analyst demonstrated how she had made the city into a kind of womb. He pointed out that she had not told him about the man she lived with, nor even the name of the restaurant where she worked. She admitted that she had been aware of her secrecy about the outside world, especially the restaurant. She described the restaurant as being in a basement, and that it looked like a dark tunnel, a womb symbol. "I carry a dark pit with me, I carry a bag with me, and I don't want you to come in," she explained. Growing more anxious, she began to scream, "It's so silly, so silly! But I can't tell you the name of the restaurant! If I tell you, you will come in. If you come in, I'll throw you out; I'll kill you!"

The analyst neither encouraged nor discouraged her to tell him the name or location of the restaurant. He allowed her to maintain her own pace regarding this issue. For some days she cried and said things like: "If you come in, I'll melt. I'll be liquid. You are Mafia! If you come in, you'll shoot me. You don't know, but I have been living in anxiety for months that one day you would walk into that restaurant. You will come in and *bug* me, torment me."

The day before the Thanksgiving separation from the analyst, she reported a dream in which she found herself in a building. "I was inside, way inside," she said. "The walls were soft and puffy, like cotton." She associated this with being in a womb. The puffy walls also reminded her of the puffy clouds in her conscious fantasy of flying through such clouds in an airplane, the fantasy that she reported during the initial part of her analysis. The day residue came from her having gone to a store and seen and heard a crying child. Suddenly she sensed that as a child she herself had cried to exhaustion, feeling badly hurt, when her brothers' births and her mother's illnesses had caused her such intolerable traumas. This was why she wanted to "regress" into her mother's womb. She screamed that being in the womb no longer satisfied her, and that she wanted to get out but was still frightened. At the next session after the Thanksgiving holiday, she reported a dream about herself. "A woman who looked like a reptile swam to the shore out of dark waters. There was sunshine. The reptile was me; I felt good, but if I am outside the womb they'll know I am not a nice little girl. I am angry!''

At the next session, she screamed at the analyst, "Hurt me, push and prod me so I will tell you the name of the restaurant!'' The analyst interpreted that Lisa was assuming a masochistic position and asking her analyst to be a sadist, because she perceived the idea of separation from the mother (swimming out of her womb) as an act of aggression.

As this month came to an end Lisa reported dreaming of "this weird man. If he saw me he would kill me. I went into a room, it was my mother's bathroom, and hid in the bathtub in the water. The bottom of the bathtub was pink, and I put a pink towel on so that I could really hide. A woman and David came in. The woman noticed me but said nothing. Then they left. I came out of the bathtub but hid in the curtains as if I had become one of the curtains of soft material.'' Lisa interpreted the dream herself by saying that she had been hiding in her mother's womb. She herself was also the woman with David, observing her regressive self but doing nothing. "I wanted to be gotten by this weird man, who was you, and be brutalized,'' she said. "It is perverted. But if I am brutalized I would experience sadness, and not feel angry and guilty, and I will leave my cloudy world.''

She now realized that she was really afraid of her rage against her sibling representations and against the mother's representation. Because of her rage the idea of separating from her mother (her womb) was like murdering her. This was why she demanded that the analyst punish and brutalize her. She added: "I see a little girl in a rage. But I am not ready to say it is me.''

December

She began her first hour in December by saying that she was flooded with images and dreams of being in a womb. "I feel sick and guilty,'' she said. In one dream she saw the restaurant, "a womblike place,'' where around a table sat little ratlike animals. They wore uniforms as though they were from VMI (Virginia Military Institute). In reality at VMI the first-year cadets are called *Brother Rats*. The animals in the restaurant represented Lisa's siblings (the brothers). VMI also stood for "*Volkan, Mother*, and *I*.''

Addressing the analyst she said, "The issue about my mother's pregnancies is now between us," and added, "Somehow we'll resolve this issue." At the end of the hour she began to cry and said that something was leaving her but she would not die by losing it. "It feels like a passage," she added. "I feel like going somewhere, standing alone, and telling myself that I am in charge. I'll take charge—gather myself." As her crying continued, she went on, "I want to be close to you." The analyst suggested that this idea frightened her, that the notion of closeness to the analyst might equate to a repetition of the type of "closeness" she had experienced with her mother. She felt frustrated because she could not maintain a sense of genuine closeness to her mother. So she symbolically entered into her mother's womb in her fantasies in order to hold onto an illusion that she would never be frustrated. She replied, "I want a different closeness with you [Dr. Volkan]. A friendship—no merging!"

The next day Lisa reported a new dream in which she saw a road sign: "Postpartum Highway." She thought that after delivering each of her babies her mother had suffered from depression. The analyst agreed with her conclusion about her mother's postpartum depressions.

As Christmas approached, Lisa discussed whether or not she was obliged to visit her mother during the holidays, or whether she might go with David to visit his family, who lived some distance away. She decided to go with David, and she was surprised that her mother did not object to her plan.

Soon thereafter she brought in a dream of ice-skating, in which a man (who stood for the analyst, she said), was teaching her to skate and to be free. She had driven in snow to get to her session, and as she got closer she felt more secure. She described the sense of security as a different kind of closeness—one that reminded her of holding her father's hand on a sunny day, feeling good inside as she walked alongside him. "I was a little girl with my father," she said. The analyst became a "good father" in the transference. He felt that this development reflected Lisa's wish to find a "good" oedipal father who would help her to separate and individuate from her mother and her womb. After speaking affectionately about Dr. Volkan as a man, Lisa also spoke of their separation at Christmas; she announced that "analysis is not the only thing in the world'' and that she would be all right during this separation.

During the last session before Christmas vacation she said, "I saw my brothers in a womb. They were not scary anymore." Her brothers had again been rats in her dream. "In the latter part of the dream the rats were just born, no fur; they were just pink. I could look at them and accept them without anxiety."

At the time they parted for this Christmas, Lisa still had not disclosed the name or location of her restaurant. During the following months she returned to reading about the habits of wolves, learning by analogy that one can live with siblings without killing them. One day she declared that the secrecy of the restaurant had lost its magic, so she told the analyst its name and location.

HARBOR OF KYRENIA

Toward the end of her third year of analysis, Dr. Volkan hung in his office a new painting that showed the harbor of Kyrenia in Cyprus, which he considers, for personal emotional reasons, one of the most beautiful spots on earth. Colorful and lively, the picture had been painted by his niece, who had given it to him on one of his visits to his homeland, Northern Cyprus. When Lisa began taking an interest in it, she showed uncanny perception by connecting it to her analyst's personal background. One day, after she asked about the painting, he found himself explaining, with some excitement in his voice, that it was the harbor of Kyrenia in Cyprus, and that it was a place he liked very much. Although Lisa had been told when referred to him that Dr. Volkan is a Cypriot Turk, she had shown no interest in his accent and given no other acknowledgment of his being an immigrant in the United States, until the painting caught her attention.

The analyst does not habitually make disclosures about himself to his patients. It was most unusual for him to have made the remark he did about the painting, disclosing as he did his affection for the place. After the session, he sought the meaning of this unusual happening. He believed that at one level the harbor picture represented his "womb," and he might well have wanted to show his patient that he had a better womb—to compare with the one in which Lisa wanted to stay even though she feared drowning or suffocating there.

FOLLOW-UP

This summary of a part of Lisa's psychoanalysis has omitted those aspects that did not relate specifically to our topic of sibling experiences. Her treatment covered a period of six years wherein she successfully resolved her many problems. They included preoedipal object-relations conflicts and the influence of the enveloped "psychotic core." She also worked on her internal response to the abandonment by her father and her pyschosexual difficulties. After getting well Lisa and David moved to another city where he attended a professional school and she worked as an elementary schoolteacher. At the school she learned fondness for small children, and to demonstrate her love for them. She prepared herself for motherhood and married David. A few years later she wrote to the analyst asking for his assistance. It turned out that she and David could not have a child. They had gone to an adoption agency, where they were asked if they had ever had psychiatric problems. Since she was honest, Lisa responded in the affirmative. The agency told them that they could not work with the couple unless they received a letter from her psychiatrist regarding her mental health. Lisa asked Dr. Volkan to write a letter on her behalf. He wrote to the agency stating that Lisa was fully analyzed and that she was a healthy woman. The analyst, however, wondered to himself if Lisa's inability to get pregnant might relate to some unresolved aspects of her unconscious fantasies. Upon adopting a son Lisa notified the analyst and thanked him for his help, including in her letter a picture of the baby they had successfully adopted. Three years later, she sent another picture of this child sitting next to a new baby. In a note Lisa informed the analyst that she had given birth to the new baby. After all, she had managed to get pregnant. Her pleasure in her life communicated itself in her note.

6 TO KILL OR TO REPAIR

This chapter examines what happens to the older child, *in adulthood,* when the intruder, the new sibling, has a birth defect or physical or emotional illness. Lisa's brothers Joe and Mark (see previous chapter) were physically healthy individuals. Dr. Albert's brother (see chapter 2) was ill. Both Lisa and Dr. Albert reacted strongly to their respective younger siblings. Interactions with mental representations of her brothers preoccupied Lisa's adult life while Dr. Albert identified disruptively with the representation of his brother. Here we ask the following question: If the new sibling is handicapped, how does this influence the way the sibling experience "settles in" to the adult mind?

The case of Mira, which we present in some detail in this chapter, demonstrates how an older sibling's disturbing symptoms and character traits related directly to her experience of having a mongoloid younger brother. In Mira we also see attempts at sublimations. If her sublimations had prevailed, Mira's adult internalized relationship with her brother's representation might have led to a positive outcome. So, to begin to answer our question we must focus on what an individual does, in adulthood, with the mental representation of a handicapped younger sibling. As Lisa's case illustrated, one does not need to have a handicapped younger sibling in order to have disturbing symptoms and character traits. The older child's projections of murderous and other negative impulses in fact, psychologically speaking, can make the younger sibling "defective" even if in reality this sibling is healthy. However, if the younger sibling really has a handicap there occurs a "fit" between the older child's projections and the actual deformity in the younger child. Working through and resolving the effects of projection, then, can become difficult. In the case of an actually handicapped sibling, the sibling's representation may play a key role in the analysis of the adult older sibling. We might refine our original question to ask: What kind of mental representation does the healthy child create for his or her "damaged" sibling, what unconscious fantasies accompany the healthy child's interaction with such a mental representation, and how do such unconscious experiences settle in to the adult mind?

LITERATURE ON HANDICAPPED CHILDREN

The mental representation of the damaged younger brother or sister sometimes appears in reports of *adults* in analysis as a factor in the formation of certain symptoms or character traits; for example, see Leaff (1984). We could not find, however, an in-depth and systematic psychoanalytic study of this topic. Most studies pertaining to handicapped siblings focus on the observable reactions of healthy children to defective or physically ill siblings; these studies do not discern between older or younger siblings. The following are examples.

Lidz and his associates (Lidz, Fleck, Alanen, and Cornelison, 1963; Lidz, Fleck, and Cornelison, 1965; and Titelman and Nilsson, 1992) reported on siblings' reactions to having schizophrenic siblings. Bergman and Wolfe (1971) studied the influence of chronically ill children on healthy siblings and stressed the resentment felt by the healthy siblings because their mothers paid more attention to the sick children. Binger (1973) reported on the emotional impact on healthy children who had siblings suffering from childhood leukemia. Trevino (1979) discussed siblings of mentally retarded children. Trevino observed that the young healthy child initially plays with his mentally retarded sibling. However, as he grows older, the healthy child assumes a superordinate position and intensifies his sibling rivalry. Sensing parental ambivalence toward the handicapped child also intensifies the healthy child's sibling rivalry. Colonna (1981) wondered about the impact of blind children on sighted siblings, and Kennedy (1985) described the case of 12-year-old David, whose difficulties in interacting with his mental representation of a handicapped brother made him feel like a "replacement child," interfered with his assertiveness, and affected his transition through the oedipal phase (see Introduction).

The grieving of parents with a defective or ill child received attention by psychoanalysts such as Solnit and Stark (1961). Some mothers concentrate their devotion on the handicapped child and neglect the healthy ones, while others may turn away from the "damaged" child (Colonna and Newman, 1983). Mintzer, Als, Tronick, and Brazelton (1984) studied parents in five families who had first-born infants with visible birth defects. All of these parents, in their thirties and moderately well educated, went through a grieving process. Mintzer and his colleagues describe three stages that parents traverse in adjusting to having children with birth defects: (1) an initial sense of shock, disappointment, anger, and injury to self-esteem; (2) a period of painful intrapsychic disequilibrium; and, (3) the gradual restoration of psychic equilibrium. Clearly, the parents cannot escape reacting to having a "damaged" child. The nature of and complications in their grief in turn influence the reactions of their healthy children toward the defective or ill sibling.

In spite of the availability of studies about healthy siblings' reactions to handicapped siblings, Colonna and Newman's (1983) review of this topic suggested that this area required further study. An examination of the literature published since their review shows that this topic has still received little attention by psychoanalysts.

A HANDICAPPED INTRUDER

The following detailed study describes a patient's mental representation of her younger sick sibling as it existed in her adult internal world. We will show how the patient sometimes identified with the sick sibling's representation and at other times interacted with it as a separate object representation, experienced internally or externally. The patient, whom we call Mira, also had unconscious fantasies accompanying her identifications and relationships with her sick brother's representation.

Mira was an 18-year-old high school student when she became Dr. Ast's patient. As she began analysis, she had suffered from abdominal pain for two years, and had received treatment from an internist for the pain. Having made no progress in diagnosing the pains in nearly a year, the physician finally performed a colonoscopy to "look into" Mira's intestines (belly). As we will show, "looking into" a belly had significant symbolic meaning for Mira. We think that she had played a role in convincing the physician to perform such a task. In any case, the physician, finding nothing physically wrong in Mira's intestines, diagnosed her as suffering from psychosomatic symptoms, and referred her to analysis. Mira, however, waited for a year before starting. We focus here on *selected* aspects of Mira's case in order to illustrate how a mongoloid younger brother's representation in Mira's internal world and her interactions and identifications with it led to the conflicts and anxieties that underlay some of Mira's thinking, action, and repeated behavioral patterns. This case also gives examples of Christmas "neurosis" and animal symbolism.

Mira's Background

Mira was the first child of a middle-class family. Her parents had been married for 10 years and they had hoped to have a child earlier, but her mother did not conceive one until Mira. At the time of Mira's birth, however, the marriage had problems. Soon after her birth, her mother periodically wanted to separate from her father, but the parents did not get a divorce. Then, under strained marital conditions, the mother became pregnant again. During the last part of the pregnancy the mother sensed that something was wrong with the fetus. She often pressed her abdomen to elicit a response from the baby she carried, and sometimes she thought that the unborn baby was dead. Eventually she gave birth to a son, Bernd, when Mira was 2 years old. The father, who had wanted a son, was horrified because Bernd was severely lethargic at birth and diagnosed as mongoloid; he clearly needed extreme care. For example, he could not swallow properly, and the parents had to feed him in a certain way every two hours to compensate for his problem. If he was ever to walk, they had to give him physical therapy several hours a day from the first month of life onward.

After birth Bernd had to remain hospitalized intermittently for a year and finally was brought home for good on a December 24th, when Mira was celebrating her third Christmas. The parents' marriage still had problems (the father continued to have liaisons with other women), but they decided to remain together as a family and keep Bernd at home. Soon after Bernd's return from the hospital, the family moved to a new location specially built to house families with handicapped children. They lived there for a couple of years. Mira's initial response to the new situation can be seen in her identification, or at least her attempt at identification, with her brother (and perhaps with the "sick child" representations of other handicapped children in that location): she did things in order to receive the same kind of special attention they received from the adults. She hurt herself "every day" and even had to visit the hospital for a variety of problems, some of which required minor surgery.

At the age of 3 she managed to injure her head badly. Apparently she bled profusely making her parents fear severe damage. Later Mira recalled this incident with a sense of "pride." Her being "proud" of having a damaged head was due to its allowing her to join ranks with a handicapped brother and receive special attention. It is interesting that Mira's father also managed to hurt his head during the same time period, by hitting it on an iron bar while exercising. It seems that he too, for his own reasons, might have wished to identify with his mongoloid son. In any case, Mira's father joined his daughter in making a big fuss about her head trauma. He began joking that Mira had a "damaged roof," a German expression roughly equivalent to "having rocks in one's head." Mira had many accidents later on, including at age 8 a life-threatening chest injury after a fall from a horse.

When Mira was 5 years old she began having daydreams in which she was a princess and her parents (who were preoccupied with Bernd) were not her real parents. This conscious fantasy remained with her until age 12, but it did not adequately soothe her narcissistic hurts.

Eventually the family moved to a new location leaving behind the place where many handicapped children lived. But, Bernd, of course, needed further medical attention. Mira often accompanied her mother as she took Bernd to the various therapeutic services he required. She observed her brother in play therapy, speech therapy, and so on. Sometimes she sat with her mother behind a one-way mirror observing her brother on the "central stage," while she stayed on the "outside." To become an insider she had to identify with her brother. At times her identification with him reached near-perfection! When she started school, Mira could not learn to read, write, or speak clearly—as though she herself had a mental disability. Her parents took her to specialists and arranged for language lessons for her, which accomplished her goal of receiving special treatment like a handicapped child. She remembered the doctor visits and language lesson days as "wonderful days." She told Dr. Ast how these activities always took place on days full of sunshine, reflecting the gratification provided by her identification with a handicapped sibling. After school Mira could not do her homework alone. She would cling to her mother and both of her parents believed she truly had a learning disability. Of course, this proved untrue. When Mira went through the adolescent passage and "reexamined" (unconsciously) her own and others' mental representations, she transformed into an excellent student, having partially thrown away her "handicapped" self representation. Later, for psychological reasons she began once more not to succeed in school, as we will describe shortly.

To complicate her identification and attempts at identification with a mongoloid intruder, Mira also responded to her father's not-so-hidden disappointment in his son. Mira's father had wanted a son, but Bernd clearly did not fulfill his father's expectations. Perhaps her father had fantasies about Mira being handicapped instead of Bernd. The father's fantasy-wish might have dovetailed with Mira's fantasy-wish to get attention by "being" or appearing damaged. Alongside this possibility, Mira's father also clearly wished for the other side of this coin—that Mira, the healthy child, was a boy. For example, when she was 6 years old, he stopped her from practicing ballet and encouraged her to play soccer. In response, she became a "tomboy." In her treatment it became clear that her negotiation of the Oedipus complex did not go in the expected direction. Instead of pleasing her father by acting feminine, she pleased him by acting masculine. Aspects of this personality trait remained with Mira until some time into her treatment with Dr. Ast.

Aggression and Murder Attempts

Attempts at identification with a mongoloid or a healthy boy image were two ways that Mira unconsciously adapted to having a handicapped brother, "losing" her parents, and having to compensate for her father's disappointment in his son. But such attempts alone did not assuage her feelings, especially her aggressive feelings. Her mother could not help her to tame her aggression and feel comfortable with it. Her mother would not talk to her daughter if Mira treated Bernd badly. Once little Mira wrote a letter to her mother asking for her forgiveness and wishing that her mother would talk to her again. But instead of understanding Mira's dilemma her mother corrected Mira's grammar! Thus the direct expression of aggression would lead to the "loss" of mother's love. Mira then either had to turn her aggression to herself or project it to the environment, but away from Bernd and her mother. Such projections provided temporary relief, but they often backfired and scared her.

Sometimes her projected aggression seemingly took on a life of its own, and boomeranged back to her. For example, when finding herself in disagreement with other children or in fights with them, she would see skulls coming out of walls and think of her bed as made of a bunch of snakes. She perceived a picture of Jesus in her room as someone consisting of "scary eyes." In her treatment she recalled childhood thoughts that baby Bernd, like the Jesus she envisioned, consisted only of eyes, and that he could communicate through his eyes. (Bernd never learned to speak properly.) "Bad" brother and "bad" Jesus condensed in her mind. It is not clear if her visions of skulls and eyes were

nightmares or hallucinations. Mira, however, did not develop full-
blown schizophrenia.

When Mira was 4 years old she hit a neighborhood boy with
an iron bar on the head while they were "playing." (It should be
recalled that Mira's father's head was injured when he hit his
head on an iron bar. Besides wanting to kill her sibling, we suggest
that Mira also wanted to express aggression toward her oedipal
father who wanted a son and not a girl.) The boy was younger
than she by a year. He fell down unconscious, his head bleeding.
She felt temporarily triumphant and happy to see this, but she
immediately feared getting caught. She managed to change her
attitude, look for help, and become "caring" toward the injured
boy, who was taken to the hospital. Mira received compliments
from the adults for her "helpful attitude" toward the injured boy.
She told everyone that the injury resulted from an accident, but
feared that the boy would tell the truth when he regained consciousness. In Mira's adult recollection of this incident, she
thought that she had stayed by his bedside for hours, and managed to be in the hospital when he regained consciousness.
Whether or not her recollection is factually accurate, it certainly
reflects her anxiety and her defenses against it. She also thought
that after he awoke she had bribed him with a promise of a gift
if he did not inform others about her role in the whole thing.
She related how she and her father, in whom Mira had confided
about the truth of the injury, had later taken a toy to the boy.

When Mira was 5 years old her mother became pregnant
again. Mira accompanied her mother when she visited her obste-
trician. Mira was allowed to see the ultrasound images of the
fetus in her mother's belly. Seeing her mother's swollen belly and
recalling the images of her insides, Mira had conscious fantasies
of her mother's belly exploding. However, her mother's belly did
not explode, and she had a new baby. This sibling, a sister, was
normal. For a while, though, Mira unconsciously transferred her
aggressions from Bernd to this sister. After all, the new baby, like
her mongoloid brother, might ruin her life! The day before her
baby sister was to be baptized, Mira dropped her "by accident"
while carrying her. This was her second "murder" attempt. The
baby's skull fractured and she had to stay in the hospital for several weeks. Mira, much older now than when Bernd arrived, had

real potentiality to kill her new sibling who, in her mind, could do to her what Bernd had done.

This "murder attempt" still did not adequately express her feelings about Bernd and the newest intruder into her family, it apparently scared Mira so much that she decided never to be angry with her mongoloid brother again! We see here the beginning of her reaction formation or attempted sublimation; it continued in her adulthood work as a caregiver for sick people, as we will report. But, of course, one cannot stop murderous rage and associated unconscious fantasies by conscious decisions, nor can one control the effectiveness and reliability of reaction formations or sublimations.

During her late latency age, Mira and her classmates visited the former concentration camp, Dachau, where they heard about Nazis and what they had done to mentally ill and handicapped people. Mira listened with attention as she heard how the Nazis would have treated someone like her brother. These "undesirable" individuals were systematically killed to unencumber the healthy people, who would then be free to devote more energy to useful work. Mira interpreted that this would allow healthy children to have the benefit of better maternal care. Her father told her about another Nazi policy: that if any family hid a damaged child, the whole family would be punished. Around this time, Mira also watched a documentary about Pompeii. In this documentary, the reconstructed faces of mummified corpses in the ruins looked like "the living dead." Watching the film made Mira extremely anxious. Her unconscious fantasy that she had "killed" Bernd and that the "living dead" would return to take revenge appeared symbolically in the way Mira described these two events (the visit to Dachau and watching the documentary on Pompeii) in analysis.

Adolescent Passage

Earlier we wrote about Mira becoming an excellent student while she went through adolescence. But this change was one of only a very few positive modifications that she managed to make during this critical phase of development, when a youngster has the potential to change her character traits and solidify her identity (Blos, 1979). Another positive development involved turning to music. She composed songs, played the music, and sang the songs for many hours of the day, as though creating a mother who sang lullabies to soothe her anxieties. A woman music teacher would allow her to play the piano and express herself without using sheet music. Sometimes Mira's "music" was chaotic and unstructured.

In spite of these attempts at modifying her world, however, going through the adolescent passage did not change the characteristics of Mira's personality. In fact, traumatic events during this period made her passage more difficult and helped to crystallize in her mind that abandonments and frustrations would continue to plague her. One of these events was being fondled sexually by some adults in her neighborhood while visiting them. This fascinated, but also humiliated her. She was humiliated by thinking of herself as a "stupid little girl" for allowing the fondling to occur. In her analysis she understood that her humiliation by the neighbors was condensed with her sense of humiliation about having a mongoloid brother.

The other event was the death of her paternal grandfather, who had had a stabilizing effect on Mira. To make matters worse, right after her grandfather died, her mother entered the hospital for hip surgery and stayed there for six months, and her father became depressed. The environment during Mira's adolescent passage was not conducive to her making adaptive modifications, and in fact during this period in her life Mira experienced some depression.

The Death of a Black Cat and Unconscious Womb Fantasies

At the age of 13, Mira got a male black cat. During her treatment it became clear that the black cat represented her own depressed self as well as the "bad" mongoloid brother whom she wanted to "love" and to change. Mira used the cat as an attempt to split and externalize her troublesome self and object representation. Mira often "talked" to the cat as if he were a person. But one day the cat was poisoned by "accident." Mira and her father took the cat to a veterinary hospital where the cat was put to death by injection, just like some victims of the Nazis were put to death—"worthless" or "sick" beings had to be destroyed! Her target of externalization gone, Mira became very disturbed. She retreated to her bedroom, asked for *pink* curtains, *pink* sheets, and *pink* paint on the walls, and her parents complied. A tree just outside the window made her room rather dark. In this dark, pink room Mira symbolically regressed to her mother's womb. Her retreating to this room reflected her unconscious fantasy of being in her mother's womb. The reader should recall similar pink images in Lisa's dreams and daydreams (chapter 5). Like Lisa, Mira felt surrounded by a cloudy atmosphere. She would walk with a shuffle and feel as though she might fall and damage her head. She also began sucking on bars of chocolate candy and became obese. We feel that Mira was enacting the roles of the various players in her most traumatic event—the birth of Bernd. She *was* Bernd when she walked like him and risked damaging her head; she *was* her pregnant mother when she grew obese. Her obesity actually helped her to enact or become Bernd as well; since he did not know how to control his eating, he too was obese. Her identifications with these various object representations were in the service of controlling the trauma of having a mongoloid brother, dealing with her aggressive impulses and conflicts, and reducing her anxiety.

Mira's main aim, like Lisa's, was to become the sole occupant of her mother's womb and symbolically kill her new sibling(s) there. Mira ignored anyone who would come into her room and she became upset if forced even to acknowledge the existence of others. She threw objects at intruders to keep them out of her room. Interestingly, when far outside of her pink room, at school, Mira now started to excel as a student. We can surmise that while at home, in her unconscious fantasy she got rid of her mongoloid brother (as well as her sister) by returning to her mother's belly. This wish satisfied, she could disidentify herself from her sick and mentally retarded brother and carry out her intellectual endeavors in an effective fashion outside of home.

Mira slowly moved out of her "womb" at the age of 16 after falling "in love" with a young man with whom she had a symbiot- iclike relationship in which they mothered each other. She also had obtained "permission" from her priest and a nun to grow up and begin to have sex. The creation of external "good" caregivers allowed her to utilize reaction formations and sublimations: for the next five years during her summer vacations she worked as a volunteer for a facility that cared for children, both severely handicapped and healthy. Her brother now attended this facility. She worked there five days a week from morning until night, "forgot" about eating, lost weight, and began to have sexual intercourse with her boyfriend. For practical purposes, she seemed outwardly a "normal" young woman.

But malignant internal processes still plagued Mira. In spite of her "goodness" and her good deeds, guilt and unconscious fantasies continued pertaining to her negative feelings about the representation of her mongoloid brother. For example, she had unwarranted fears of pregnancy, which were expressed by abdominal cramps, and often when she came down the stairs from her second-floor bedroom to the first-floor dining room to join her family for meals, she had thoughts of walking down to her execution. Such thoughts, combined with conflicts about sexuality, initiated abdominal cramps and anxiety attacks. These were the complaints that eventually led her physician to refer her to Dr. Ast.

OBSERVATIONS FROM TREATMENT

At the time that Mira came to see Dr. Ast, her mother once more had been hospitalized with hip problems, and for about a year Mira and her father looked after her mongoloid brother and her healthy sister. Her mother returned home shortly before Mira's treatment started. During the first year of her treatment Mira did not mention Bernd much. But her brother's mental representation was present in the sessions nevertheless. The analyst, for example, would sometimes feel that Mira was an extremely fragile person and that the analyst should be careful not to damage her. In retrospect the analyst realized that at such times Mira was presenting her identification with Bernd to her.

While Mira avoided references to her brother in that first year of treatment, the themes of defects in mental functions and murder appeared from the beginning. For example, she talked extensively about Kasper Hauser, a man of noble birth who had been abducted from his parents' house and confined to a basement where he had no meaningful contact with other humans during his childhood. Hauser could not talk or walk and was eventually killed. Mira also focused on the sexual abuse of her boyfriend's mother at the hands of a stepfather. This woman later married a half-brother who was accused of murder. The woman herself, according to Mira's account, had possibly murdered Mira's boyfriend's two older siblings, her own children.

Problems existed at school, too. Mira had difficulty in chemistry class because the German pronunciation of the chemical symbol for Sodium Chloride (NaCl) sounded like "Nazi." "Nazism is like chemistry," she said, "you are told something you have to believe, like the people were told to hate and dispose of Jews, and they believed in it!" References to murder were everywhere!

First Christmas While in Analysis

It should be recalled that Bernd was finally brought home after a series of long hospital stays on a December 24th, when Mira was 3 years old. During the first Christmas period after she started her analysis Mira symbolically recalled Bernd's arrival home and her subsequent sense of abandonment.

As the Christmas break came near the analyst took a brief vacation. Mira's parents, accompanied by Mira's two siblings, also took a vacation away from their home city. Mira was left behind, alone. She invited a man to her house. She knew that he trafficked in drugs and that he carried knives and a pistol in his suitcase. He raped her. The next day, she reinvited him to her house, and again, he raped her.

When they resumed their work together the analyst and Mira examined the patient's voluntary exposure of herself to danger and humiliation. Mira had felt abandoned and experienced rage which she could not express. She had created a "bad" environment as a defense against her feeling of abandonment; she had made herself the target of victimization and humiliation similar to the humiliation she had felt when her mother would prohibit

her from expressing rage and would not talk to her. Being raped
was also associated with being fondled by the neighbors, which
had made of her a "silly little 'bad' girl." By having this Christmas
experience Mira gratified herself by holding onto "objects" even
though they humiliated her, and having her analyst become a
"witness" of her victimization.

Soon after the Christmas break Mira took a class trip to Poland, where she visited Auschwitz. (It should be recalled that at
age 8 she had visited Dachau with her class.) While in Auschwitz
she felt hated and that she would be killed by the Jews also visiting
there at the time. She recalled her brother's "eyes" which she
thought communicated without using words. This trip further
reenacted certain of her recollections of her childhood. Either
she was the Jew, a victim suffering from the loss of her mother
(the analyst's absence at Christmas), or she was the Nazi, killing
deformed individuals (her brother's representation) so that she
could have her mother back and be her sole child.

Starving Bernd

Six months later Mira's parents, for the first time in twenty years,
took a two-week vacation without any of their children and left
Mira in charge of her siblings. During this period Mira decided
to starve her now 17-year-old, severely impaired mongoloid
brother. Her conscious thought was that if Bernd did not eat so
much he would lose weight and be healthier. She sent him to
school with "rotten bread." Dr. Ast heard in her attempt to "poison" Bernd an echo of the "poisoning" of her black cat. At the
last minute, her conscience bothered her. She called Bernd's
school and asked the teacher to prevent him from eating the
rotten bread.

The analyst noted that during these two weeks Mira began
perceiving and treating Bernd's fat belly as if it belonged to a
pregnant woman. Mira's associations indicated that by starving
her brother or by poisoning him she would get rid of his swollen
belly (pregnancy) and its contents (a baby).

One related incident the patient reported extended the im-
agery of pregnancy in her associations. While driving with her

brother, Mira stopped to get gasoline at a self-service station. While Mira filled the tank, Bernd asked where gasoline comes from. Filling the tank by holding a hose and having her brother in the car with her outside of it, symbolically brought to her mind a reflection of sexual intercourse and putting a baby into a womb. In associating to this incident, Mira expressed her wish to undo her mother's second pregnancy. By not feeding her brother and thereby diminishing his belly she prohibited the existence of another child in it. Then, since Mira had wished to kill her brother in her mother's belly, she felt guilty.

Dream of a Damaged Car

A dream that Mira brought to treatment further illustrates the existence and effects of her unconscious fantasy pertaining to her sibling(s) and her mother's womb. In this dream Mira drove a car, and her sister and brother were passengers. The three siblings were driving to a restaurant, but there seemed to be no way to get there. So Mira drove the car through a fence, breaking it down. A hole appeared in front of the car, the top of the car came off, and a child's bicycle at the back of the car was damaged. They arrived at the restaurant where their parents awaited them. The parents asked, "What happened?"

The car, which in actuality belonged to Mira's mother, stood for the mother's womb, with her children in it. It was ruined. It should be recalled that when Mira's mother was pregnant with Mira's sister, Mira had conscious thoughts of her mother's belly exploding. The restaurant represented parental love and narcissistic supplies for the children, and the difficulty in getting there represented Mira's sense of frustration in obtaining them.

In her dream, Mira feared the projected aspects of her aggression; while ripping through the fence she saw ugly, repulsive faces (her projected aggression) watching her. Her parents' question, "What happened?" indicated their ignorance of Mira's internal struggles; their comment denied knowledge of their own role in their children's problems. In reality, too, her mother could not empathize with Mira's dilemmas. The mother "supported" Mira's seeing the analyst by saying that 70 percent of people who have handicapped siblings have psychological problems. Her comment dismissed Mira to a small "number" among many individuals with a similar fate.

The dream made Mira very anxious. She seemed unready to work with it. Instead, she created another "womb" which she could control. She turned to her piano and like Lisa (see chapter 3), she used it as a womb where she controlled the "noises" (of babies) in it. Frequent playing soothed her anxiety.

Mira projected aspects of her conflicts onto others instead of onto members of her family or her analyst. For example, Mira struggled with a teacher whom she considered abusive of her human rights (i.e., Mira's right not to "lose" her mother through abandonment). She also brought in the plots of various movies in which killings or dead siblings appeared. Whenever she came close to sensing her murderous rage she would increase her activities of "caring" for the handicapped or playing the piano and avoid fully experiencing her rage.

Second Christmas

Mira's second Christmas in treatment reminds us of Boyer's (1955, 1985) formulations about this holiday (see chapter 2). Mira became severely depressed and wished to move to a faraway place so that she would not "kill" Bernd. However, since she chose as her destination South Africa, where apartheid, a form of "Nazism," still existed, she could not escape from her unconscious aggressive wish.

During this cold winter, her father had assigned Bernd the task of clearing snow from the roof of their garage. "By accident" Bernd fell from the roof and broke his back. Fortunately (or unfortunately, according to Mira's unconscious), he escaped paralysis, but had to stay in the hospital for over a month. Now Mira could not avoid knowing about her murderous rage. It had almost "killed" her brother! After this event she searched for a lesbian relationship, which her analyst understood as her attempt to merge (be symbiotic) with another female (her mother/analyst) and lose her individuality—and her murderous rage. When she did not succeed, Mira once more "damaged" her head (identification with her brother) and came to her session with a small bandage on her forehead. She seemed to have been searching for proof of her oneness with hospitalized Bernd in order to prevent her aggression toward a differentiated object representation. Furthermore, if she too had injuries, her guilt would abate.

At the beginning of the New Year, Mira drank for three days and nights, and spent many hours sitting in a park where the murders of a woman and of a child had recently taken place. The rumor was that a tramp had committed the murders. Mira, dressed like a tramp, behaved as such in the park. She was reenacting aspects of her unconscious fantasy by imitating the murderer and "killing" the woman (her mother) and the child (her brother).

A Chemical Formula

Her unconscious fantasy about her mother's womb and the siblings in it also appeared in a new dream. The day's residue came from her work at a pond as part of her chemistry class. In the dream, one chemical matter was mixed with another. If the correct amount of the first matter was added, the mixture would be good and nutritious. But if too much of the first chemical was used, the mixture would be poisonous. A special instrument indicated whether the mixture turned out good or bad. If good, Mira could add it to the pond to provide nutrition for the fish, but if it turned out bad, it would poison the fish. After treating the pond with a mixture, Mira wrote a report to say that the pond was all right. However, after submitting her report, Mira realized that the pond contained poisonous water. She became very anxious and woke up.

In reality, carp lived in the pond where Mira's class had visited. Her teacher had told the class that the carp had absorbed the poisonous elements, cleaning the water. In the Fall the carp would be removed from the pond. Of course, then their bodies would contain the poison. A thought occurred to Mira: that the authorities who removed the fish might not destroy but sell them. If they did so, the fish would poison the individuals who ate them.

The story reflected Mira's concern about her ambivalence regarding her sibling(s) (the fish) and her mother's womb (pond), and her anxiety that her aggression might prevail. The poisoned fish might not be destroyed, and through eating them (introjection and identification) she might poison or harm herself. There seemed to be no way to avoid the effect of her aggression, it might boomerang! Her one hope was the instrument (the analyst, the analytic process) which would measure her mixing of libido (nurturing element) and aggression (poisonous element) and thus "neutralize" her aggression (Hartmann, 1939).

Another association to this dream was Mira's recollection of an aquarium at her kindergarten. Some aggressive children had smashed it, seemingly without anxiety. Mira recalled feeling envious of them. She wished that she could join them. The dream itself and her associations to it allowed further progress toward neutralizing Mira's aggression.

Separation Reaction

Still in the second year of her analysis, Mira had a most interesting reaction to her analyst's one-month separation from her. This time her internalized interaction with her childhood environment came to life with full force. But now Mira had a better observing ego. As the separation from Dr. Ast approached, Mira graduated from high school. The same day, her parents, lacking any sensitivity, left home for a holiday taking her two siblings with them. They had chosen this particular time because her brother's school was closed during this period. Once more Bernd's welfare had come first, and Mira was left alone at a time when she needed acknowledgment and celebration for her achievement. As a response to this trauma, which brought to mind her childhood traumas, Mira "killed" Dr. Ast by missing one of the sessions just prior to the anticipated absence. She gave as a reason that she had injured her leg. Once more her guilt feelings might have led to her accident, but even without this self-injuring behavior, she would also have identified with the damaged brother who was the center of attention once again.

Just before the analyst's vacation started, Mira dreamt about snakes. Two of them (two siblings) went into Mira's vagina and came out of her mouth and lay beside her head (just like newborn babies are laid beside the head of the mother after birth). Mira also experienced "hallucinations" in which she saw many snakes. However, she kept her observing ego and recalled how she had had similar experiences as a child. She reassured her analyst that unlike what had happened in her childhood, this time the "snakes" did not seem scary; she knew she had created them in her mind. She could either watch them or make them vanish by pressing a lit cigarette on them. In discussing her dream and her "hallucinations," both the analyst and the patient felt that during the coming "rejection" by the analyst (parents), the patient had relived her childhood responses to intrusion from her new siblings and, this time, tolerated them. The analyst closed her office for a month. During this time, as a reaction formation against her rage toward her mother/analyst and sibling(s), Mira began taking care of a woman with a severe physical handicap, but she allowed herself to be aware of her envy toward this woman. Mira's own leg had healed.

The Third Christmas: The "Bad" Jesus

In the third year of her analysis Mira became the girl friend of a young man with a handicapped twin sister. The twin's situation represented a "reversal" of Mira's own background: the man was healthy while the woman was handicapped. It became clear that her "choosing" to be intimate with her new boyfriend and his twin sister was loaded with psychological implications.

This relationship helped Mira to unrepress the memories of many childhood events. For example, she recalled playing "doctor games" with Bernd and wanting to cut off his penis and keep it for herself. She also recalled torturing, killing, and "raping" her dolls.

As Mira's third Christmas in analysis approached she was busy unearthing her past memories and feeling that she had a cancerous lesion (a "bad baby") in her abdomen. Now she recalled Bernd's arrival to their home the day before Christmas. Mira could see in her mind's eye a big cradle. At Christmas time the family would take this cradle out of storage and place it under the Christmas tree. A baby Jesus doll would be placed in it along with dolls of Joseph, Mary, and some animals surrounding them. The family cat sometimes would sleep there too. When Bernd was first brought to the house on a December 24th *he* was put into this cradle and under the Christmas tree. Bernd was the baby Jesus! No wonder as a child Mira was afraid of a "bad" Jesus and his eyes. Mira's early Christmases were traumatic. When she was 7 years old she asked for a pink backpack as a Christmas gift. She was given one which was red and blue. She thought that it was a backpack for boys. She was so enraged that she cut her gift into pieces and threw it away.

A few days before her third Christmas in analysis Mira had a skiing accident and came to her analyst's office on crutches. Her associations to the accident gave her further insight about her childhood reactions to Bernd/Jesus's birth and her identification with a handicapped sibling. This identification also expressed itself when Mira moved into the apartment of her boyfriend's handicapped twin. The sister had gone elsewhere and in fact Mira planned to stay in the apartment for eight months. During this time she wanted her analyst to take care of her and she grew angry when in transference the analyst represented Mira's mother, who had no time for her daughter. On the other hand, Mira herself would often take care of handicapped people. At this point in her treatment, however, this attempt at reaction formation did not succeed because Mira was now openly experiencing her rage against the representation of her handicapped brother. Thus, sometimes she entertained murderous fantasies about her handicapped charges.

TOWARD GETTING WELL

When Mira graduated from high school and began to consider her future at a university or in a workplace she faced a dilemma. At this time she was living in her own apartment. She knew that her treatment was not finished and she wished to continue working with Dr. Ast. Due to certain regulations in Germany, the analyst needed to write a document stating why Mira needed to stay in the city to attend a local university where she and the analyst could continue her treatment. This document is called an *Ortsbindungsantrag*, which roughly translates as a "location binding application." In this document the analyst wrote that if Mira stopped seeing her, the patient might lose the progress she had made in her treatment so far. The analyst also wrote that if Mira went to another city and saw another therapist, her accomplishments with Dr. Ast could not be adaptively transferred to her new therapeutic situation. Mira remained Dr. Ast's patient while waiting to apply to a university. This unusual "interference" in the analytic relationship, however, led to an intensification of Mira's transference neurosis. Now she had "concrete evidence" that her analyst-mother cared for her!

Mira's transference neurosis at this time manifested itself especially in two areas: one area involved Mira reenacting more intensely her childhood identifications with handicapped children by developing psychosomatic symptoms and/or by getting into accidents and then wanting the analyst's absolute attention. She complained that her physical pain was "under her heart" (*unter dem Herzen*). Dr. Ast reminded Mira that this phrase was also used in German for another meaning: carrying a baby [Bernd] under one's heart. When Mira did not get the absolute attention she wanted, she perceived the analyst as "bad," and became sadistic toward Dr. Ast; for example, calling her degrading names. Sometimes Mira made Dr. Ast a handicapped person by coming to her sessions late and symbolically "chopping off" part of her. She was now expressing the rage she could not express as a child. In addition, thanks to the therapeutic alliance, Mira could observe her reenactments. Once she called her mother to take her to the hospital. But after realizing that she was trying to create a caring mother for herself (by identifying with Bernd), Mira decided to go to the hospital by herself.

The second area where her transference neurosis became obvious was in Mira's wish to identify with Dr. Ast as a "good" mother. She began speaking of studying psychology and becoming a psychotherapist. But then Mira declared that to be a psychotherapist was to make oneself a target for patients' sadism. So Mira decided that she therefore would not become a therapist. Her analyst interpreted Mira's dilemma and told her that it was

Mira's own sadism and guilt that interfered with her wish to identify with a "good" mother.

As Mira began to observe more clearly the meanings of her intense transference neurosis, she felt like she was riding a roller coaster. In her sessions she would fluctuate from being "lethargic" like Bernd and "forcing" Dr. Ast to look after her, to genuinely attempting to leave her neurosis behind. When there was a question about the continuation of insurance coverage for her analysis she freely exhibited rage against the insurance company. She felt entitled to the coverage since she thought that the society should know how being raised with a defective sibling might be disastrous and should compensate her for having had to grow up with a defective sibling. Examining her own rage at having had to deal with a handicapped person in her life allowed her to develop empathy for her parents and sympathy for her brother. She told her analyst that now she often felt free of her "mongoloid world." Then she wondered if to be completely free from neurosis would be boring. After all, in spite of the extreme burden it caused, her neurosis, her preoccupation with Bernd's mental representation, had kept her busy. What would she do in a "new" non-neurotic world? She demanded a guarantee from Dr. Ast that her internal life would remain active and interesting. The analyst sensed that Mira was like a child who was learning how to walk on her own. She told Mira that a non-neurotic life might have its own cruelties, but not linking them with internal burdens would allow her to deal with such possible cruelties in adaptive ways. Also, the analyst said, there were no rules saying that a non-neurotic life must be dull. After this Mira went skiing, enjoyed her activity, and did not have an accident.

Having developed a positive transference toward her analyst Mira now began to work on oedipal themes. Because of the untamed aggressions of her childhood, in her mind she had mixed sexuality with aggression. For example, in her unconscious, sexual relationships were associated with stories of Blue Beard who would mutilate and kill his mates. Sibling death wishes were condensed with oedipal themes.

One day Mira brought a newly completed painting to her analyst. It clearly represented her "former mongoloid world." It showed a desert shadowed by shady figures. "This was my land,"

Mira said, and indicated her readiness to leave it behind. The next day she had a dream in which shadowy figures were departing from her body.

7 DEPOSITED REPRESENTATIONS

So far in this book we have focused on the older sibling's reactions to a new sister or brother and how these reactions appear in the older siblings' internal worlds when they are adults. Occasionally similar reactions may occur in the minds of the younger children; for example, a younger child may be influenced by the experience of having a defective or ill older sibling. Is there a condition which affects the "intruder," the new sibling, more usually than it affects the older child? Volkan's (1981, 1987) concept of "deposited representations" explains an interesting phenomenon that more often than not happens to the younger rather than the older child, "settling in" to his mind as this child slowly becomes an adult. This concept refers to a type of transgenerational transmission, where a parent or other important individual deposits into a child's developing self representation a preformed self or object representation that comes from the older individual's mind.

There are various types of deposited representations. For example, an individual experiences a traumatic event in which he suffers drastic losses, such as the death of loved ones or the loss of land. At the same time he feels helpless, ashamed, and humiliated. Because the person is traumatized and the losses are great, he cannot effectively mourn the loss and move on. Furthermore, he cannot reverse the feelings of helplessness, shame, and humiliation. Individuals differ in their ways of handling traumatic situations; some predominantly use externalization as a defense mechanism. One of Dr. Ast's patients, a young man, was traumatized by two surgeries on his penis at the ages of 5 and 10 respectively. After his first surgery his father implied that now he had a castrated son. The patient was extremely humiliated, and even though his penis was now functional, in his mind's eye he perceived himself as less than a man. When he became an adult he worked in an orthopedic hospital as an orderly. His analysis revealed that the "crippled" persons in this hospital represented the patient's "castrated" self. The patient, in a sense, "enveloped" and externalized his unwanted part onto others. Now, however, he was doomed to look after his externalized self and control it. Thus, his work as an orderly in the orthopedic hospital was not a choice, it was a compulsion.

The above case vignette clearly illustrates how a person "envelopes" and externalizes an unwanted aspect of himself. What interests us here is that sometimes the individual "envelopes" his traumatized self representation and externalizes it into the developing self representation of a child. This is what we call a deposited self representation. Then in his interactions with the child, the adult sends "messages" so that now it becomes the child's task to deal with the traumatized self representation of the older person. The child has to do the mourning and reverse the unpleasant affects. He may or may not be successful in doing this. The transaction just described results in the transgenerational transmission of a trauma, where one generation passes a traumatized representation to someone in the next generation.

For example, Volkan and Ast (1994) described the case of a man they call Peter the Hunter. Peter's biological father left the family when the boy was a few weeks old. As an infant and small child Peter was raised by his mother and grandmother who were angry at men. They took out their anger on Peter. They overfed him, for example, and made him a fat boy. When Peter was 4 years old, a man entered into his life, by becoming Peter's mother's boyfriend and later marrying her. This man had been involved in the Baatan Death March and had spent years in a Japanese prison camp in the Philippines. Volkan and Ast explain in detail how the older man "deposited" his humiliated "imprisoned" self into the little boy and then proceeded, mostly through nonverbal means, to repair this injured self, now within the boy. Thus, the boy grew up to become a hunter—but not a sportsman. Whenever his self-esteem was severely threatened he would machine gun a herd of deer, for example. The message that Peter received was that it was better to be a hunter than to be hunted. By hunting Peter attempted to reverse his stepfather's experiences in the Philippines condensed with his own childhood "imprisonment" by the women.

So far we have briefly described how one's "enveloped" *self* representation can be externalized into a developing child's self representation. For our purpose here we will focus on a particular kind of *object* representation that can be deposited into a developing child's self representation. In this instance, the already formed object representation which exists in the mind of an older individual represents that person's dead or dying child, for whom the adult could not properly mourn. When a new child is introduced into the older person's environment, by birth or adoption, this child may become the reservoir of the deposited object representation, which is usually idealized. As he grows the child may be able to assimilate and integrate this deposited representation into his total self representation. In this case an identification occurs, but it is an unusual type of identification. Normally, it is the child's ego's task to accomplish an identification even when this task is influenced by the realistic or fantasized relationship with that person. When the child identifies with a deposited representation of a dead or dying sibling, the object representation of that sibling is *forced* into the child's self representation. The dominant influence on the child to form this type of identification comes from outside; for example, his grieving mother who in her interaction with her new child influences the child to assimilate and thus keep "alive" the dead child's representation.

If, on the other hand, the developing child only partially assimilates the deposited representation and cannot integrate it with the rest of his self representation, he will have a split in his total self representation and may develop a condition such as a borderline or narcissistic personality organization, in which the splitting of the self representation is a prominent feature (Volkan, 1987; Volkan and Ast, 1994). This inability to integrate and adjust internally to a deposited object representation may even result in the formation of a psychotic condition.

In the psychoanalytic literature the concept of the deposited representation of a dead or dying sibling is associated with the better known term *replacement child.* While the term replacement child mostly refers to observable phenomena, such as a mother naming her younger child after her dead child or the younger child already having a "past history," the concept of deposited representation allows us to investigate internal structural processes. In adults we may see the remains of the deposited representation and how it, along with the unconscious fantasies which are associated with it, has influenced the development of the personality organization, personality traits, and symptoms.

REPLACEMENT CHILDREN AND BEYOND

There is a permeability between the psychic boundaries of the very young child and his mother (or other important individual) that lasts beyond the symbiotic stage, and this permeability allows various "psychic contents" to pass from one to the other's self representation. For example, affects often pass through the psychic boundaries of the mother and the child. One of the most important clinical contributions of Sullivan (1962) was his study on the way in which a mother's anxiety is conveyed to her child. This process had been graphically exemplified in Anna Freud's and Dorothy Burlingham's (1942) observation of children in England during World War II. They found that, under the hazardous conditions that then prevailed, the young child reflected the anxiety of an anxious mother or caregiver. Significantly, they noted that if very young children were not separated from their mother or mother substitutes, and if these women were not anxious, their children were not traumatized by repeated exposure to bombing.

There are countless clinical vignettes in the literature that show the affective flow between the early mother and her child. Mahler's (1968) observations concerning the symbiotic phase of child development indicate that the early mother and her child function almost as one psychological unit. We have already illustrated (see chapter 1), with reference to a transsexual patient, how unconscious fantasies can be transmitted to the developing child by an older person (also see: Volkan and Masri, 1989; Volkan, 1995; Volkan and Greer, 1996). In the case of the transgenerational transmission of self or object representations, both affects and unconscious fantasies attach themselves to the deposited representations. Now, let us focus specifically on sibling representations as deposited representations. First, we will review what has been said about "replacement children" in the literature dealing with children.

Several authors have noted that after the death of a child, a mother who has been guilt-ridden, depressed, phobic, or compulsive may replace her lost child with another who still lives, an assignment likely to cause psychological difficulties for the living surrogate (Cain and Cain, 1964; Legg and Sherick, 1976; Ainslie and Solyom, 1986). Poznanski (1972) elaborates the potential hazards for the substitute child, offering the case of Susie and her observable symptoms as an example. Susie was a 15-year-old girl whose family had considered her a replacement for a dead sibling. "Replacing a child with another allows the parents partially to deny the first child's death. The replacement child then acts as a barrier to the parental acknowledgment of death, since a real child exists who is a substitute" (Poznanski, 1972, p. 1193). But Susie herself could not escape the idea of death that had been imposed upon her. Her mind and life-style seemed to focus on death-related topics; she not only had nightmares about death but acquired a boyfriend who actually attempted to kill her. Susie had automatically acquired a "past history," and inherited a legend of performance and expectations generated by a child no longer alive. Poznanski considered the idealization of the dead child a typical component of the replacement child syndrome.

Green and Solnit (1964) wrote a collection of case stories about children with poorly developed psychosocial functions. Some of the children in these case stories represent a dead sibling in their parents'—especially their mothers'—eyes. Green and Solnit noted that these parents unconsciously expected the substitute child to die prematurely as well.

> [T]he child senses the mother's expectation of his vulnerability
> and accepts his mother's distorted mental images of himself. This
> is communicated in many subtle ways but mainly through the
> mother's moods and in her way of granting him autonomy and
> independence with fearful inhibiting reservations. It can also be
> observed in the mother's way of experiencing separation from the
> child [p. 64].

Susie's case and the others briefly mentioned by Green and Solnit were studied either in pediatric inpatient units or in outpatient clinics and were not subject to searching psychoanalytic scrutiny. No attempt was made to understand metapsychologically the self-concepts of these children as they related to the representations of the dead individuals whom they replaced; they may have identified with their representations in toto, or they may have simply taken in such representations in an unassimilated and unintegrated way. Kennedy (1985) suggested that her patient David became a kind of replacement child even while his handicapped brother was alive, because the parents expected David's older brother's death—and he did die during David's childhood. We do not know how the mental representations of the lost older sibling would have modified and influenced such a patient's adult internal worlds, had the sibling survived.

We do not suggest that every "replacement child" will grow up to have pathology. To measure whether a replacement child will remain "healthy" or maladaptive requires an investigation of the internal worlds of such children, to discover what have they done through childhood and adulthood with the representations which are deposited in them.

Now let us turn our attention to the psychoanalytic literature on adults who were replacement children. Leowald (1962) describes a patient whose father had interfered with his development by clinging to him excessively. The patient served as a substitute for his father's beloved brother. Nagera (1967) and Hilgard (1969) report the fascinating story of Vincent Van Gogh. The artist was born on the same day in the same month, one year after a dead sibling, and was named after this dead sibling. Van Gogh was a replacement child who often passed by his sibling's tombstone and saw his own name on it.

Pollock (1972, 1973) provides a new perspective on the case of one of the most famous patients in psychoanalytic history—Anna O (Bertha Pappenheim) (Breuer and Freud, 1893–1895). Pollock writes that Pappenheim felt herself to be a replacement for a dead sister—and, at a later point in her life, for another dead sister as well. He adds: "We know that children who are dead may remain powerfully in the mother's mind and so can become even more important rivals for the surviving sibling, who has no ability or opportunity for reality confrontation and correction of the image of the idealized dead child" (Pollock, 1972, p. 443). Agreeing with the Cains (1964) and Rogers (1966), Pollock (1972) adds that the unresolved mourning of the parents of a dead child plays a role in their establishment of another child as a replacement.

Volkan (1981) described Linda, whose father was involved in complicated mourning over the death of his 7-year-old son. Linda was a replacement child. Although Linda appeared feminine, she was a tomboy, and analysis of her tomboyish personality revealed that it was connected with her identification with the dead boy, whom she had never even seen. When Linda had a son, who was now of the third generation, she perceived him, at least for a while, as a replacement for her father's dead son. Volkan used the term *generational continuity* in describing the links among the father, his daughter, and his grandson, who were all unconsciously connected by the representation of a dead boy, the father's first child. Blum (1983) used the same term to refer to the adoptive situation.

ADOPTIVE SITUATION

Not all replacement children are the biological children of parents who experience or expect to lose an older child. The parents in mourning can adopt a child and make him a replacement child. A reading of the literature on adopted children (Weider, 1978; Brinich, 1980; Blum, 1983; Nickman, 1985; Jacobs, 1988) suggests this possibility. Often parents adopt a child when they have given up hope of conceiving one. In such conditions the adopted child might be perceived as the incarnation of fantasized offspring. But after adopting a child or children a mother may become pregnant and deliver a child. The birth of this child can be experienced as miraculous and the child then treated like a prince or princess. Jacobs (1988) analyzed two such children with adopted siblings and showed that in both cases their being "special" was immensely gratifying to them. But both of them also suffered from profound feelings of guilt because they wanted to return or send back their adopted siblings to their original homes.

Blum (1983) recognized the complex interrelationships involved in family adoptions. He states:

> The adoptive situation is intergenerational; it involves the adopted child, the adoptive and natural parents of the child, and the grandparents, namely, the parents of the adoptive parents and sometimes the parents of the biological parents. Adoptive parents and grandparents and the adopted child form a communal network of interaction, identification, conscious and unconscious conflict, fantasy, and communication which influences the entire adoptive situation [p. 162].

When the adopted child is a replacement child, he comes under the influence of not only parents, but also grandparents, whether adopted or biological. The generational continuity then becomes a more complicated process. If the parents or grandparents develop conscious or unconscious "bad seed" or "black sheep" fantasies about the adopted child, the expected generational continuity becomes "poisoned."

In this chapter we will report the case of a young woman named Frances who did not possess an integrated and cohesive self representation. The details of her full story and treatment have been published (Volkan, 1981). We have chosen certain aspects of her case for inclusion in this book because her case illustrates a combined representation of *two* different persons. She was adopted into a family when she was a few days old; and her (adopted) mother deposited into the child's self representation, (1) the representation of the mother's male sibling who died in adulthood, and (2) the representation of a fetus who would have been Frances' adopted sibling had it lived (its sex was never determined). In Frances' mother's mind the representation of her dead male sibling and her fetus were condensed and in Frances' adult mind the combination of both representations played a key role in the formation of her unintegrated personality organization and her psychotic symptoms. The deposited representation in Frances' adult mind sometimes clearly was felt within her as an introject, and at other times she externalized it; at still other times Frances identified with it. Her case clearly illustrates several variations on the "fate" of a deposited representation. This case also includes a complicated generational continuity.

AN ADOPTED WOMAN WHO COMMUNICATED WITH "SPIRITS"

Frances, a woman in her midtwenties, was tall, slim, and flat-chested, with a clumsy carriage. At their first encounter, she greeted the analyst with a forced smile, and took her place in ghostly silence. She spoke of having become aware four years earlier of presences around her, especially when she was alone in her own room. At first, what she called "the spirits" did not speak, but one night, a candle in her room "lit itself" and she felt suffused with warmth at what she interpreted as a signal that her spectral visitors were good spirits. The spirits told her that they had come to make her happy, and cautioned her to eat only what they designated as "good." They then took command of her life, counseling her when to take her vacation, when to smile, when to blow her nose, and so on. She wrote down their orders and obeyed them. Some time later, however, she began to feel that her spirits were impostors, and that they were actually messengers of the devil who had come to trick her by entering her body, and thereby conquering Frances' internal world and then the whole world. Frightened, she sought help from a religious cult that she had recently joined. A cult leader performed an exorcism for her, placing her on the floor surrounded by a circle of his followers, who loudly demanded that the devil leave her body. Although this exorcism was considered successful by those who performed it, Frances continued to feel the devil's presence. One day soon after the exorcism, she ran through the city streets in the rain half-naked "to escape from the devil," and was picked up by the police and put into a hospital.

A year later and after a second hospitalization, she was still "under the control of the spirits" when Dr. Volkan first saw her. He later learned that she had been symptomatic long before the acute illness that seemed to have begun with the visits of her spirits. She had been "very shy" in childhood and had been told by the adults around her that she was slow in her "social" development, although she did well in school. She thought of herself as unlike her peers, and felt isolated. When she went to college she was unable to associate with those she felt were compatible with her own middle-class background, and she ended up becoming the girl friend of a drug pusher and taking drugs herself.

Personal History

Frances' personal history is summarized here in an organized way although she herself conveyed the particulars in a very uneven fashion. For example, during the initial phase of her treatment, which was conducted on a four times a week basis, Frances would spend an entire session on one single detail. Finally, her story emerged.

Frances was an adopted and only child. Her adoptive mother had miscarried after a five-month pregnancy, and her physician, aware of her strong desire for a child, had arranged for her to take 4-day-old Frances home from the hospital. In fact, as we will see, the mother's "strong desire" was a psychological *need*. At this time she was in an unconscious search for a reservoir (a baby) in which she could deposit the representation of her dead brother. In addition, this woman's health was poor. After her miscarriage she had to have a hysterectomy. Since she could not expect to have a baby herself, adoption was the only means to secure the child she had to have.

After the miscarriage Frances' adoptive mother was depressed for several months, and the maternal grandmother took over the mothering of the adopted child. This older woman was also in mourning over the death of her son, the brother of Frances' adoptive mother. The grandmother joined her daughter in the effort to utilize the adopted baby as a replacement child. The complex interactions Blum (1983) described about adoptive situations were very much applicable to the interaction among several generations of this family. The mother and grandmother named the baby Frances, after the dead son and brother, Francis. The maternal grandparents lived near the patient's adoptive parents at the time. When the grandfather died, Frances was 8, and the grandmother moved into her daughter's home and continued to influence the child's development.

The dead son/brother Francis had been the younger of the two siblings. Francis was "God's gift to the world" according to his family. He became a pilot, and died in a tragic plane crash during a war. In Frances' childhood they told her: "God took him away and then He gave us you." They were conscious of making Frances a "replacement child." The grandmother even referred to Frances as a "reincarnation of Francis."

When Francis' plane crashed, two other persons were killed with him, so there were three coffins at his funeral. Since all of the bodies were badly burned, the family could not know for sure in which coffin Francis lay. During the burial the dead pilot's mother had a fantasy that her son's spirit arose from one of the coffins and flew up into heaven. She shared this conscious fantasy with her daughter.

We do not know about the internal psychological relationships between the dead pilot and his mother or about that between him and his only sibling, Frances' mother. What we do know is that the two women could not let the dead pilot "die." Immediately they started to "reincarnate" him. First, his sister found a husband, who was *also* a pilot. She became pregnant, with the conscious hope of having a male child to replace her sibling. When she miscarried Frances was available to replace the (presumably male) fetus, and thus the dead pilot. Unfortunately for Frances, what was available for adoption at that time was a female child.

Frances' mother wanted to repair her own mother's grief, by marrying a pilot and by getting pregnant. The fetus, if it had lived, could have been a suitable substitute for the dead man! Alas, Frances' mother's attempt to please her own mother did not work. All indications point to complicated generational continuity issues by the time Frances was adopted. Furthermore, Frances' mother and grandmother may have resented her for being an infant of the wrong sex, considering Frances as "bad" and perceiving the lost ("male") fetus as "good." The mother had a hysterectomy, and thus there would be no other children in the family. Frances became the sole recipient of the mother's and the grandmother's perception of her as both idealized—male (Francis/the lost fetus) and also "bad" (wrong-sexed Frances). The mother and grandmother's unconscious "bad seed" fantasy then was connected with the adopted child's representation; even the people in the older generation tried to make Frances identify with the dead pilot's representation. One can imagine the difficulty Frances faced; her circumstances made it nearly impossible to become a psychologically integrated child.

Symptoms

When Frances started her treatment the analyst did not know that she was an adopted child. The patient did not present a cohesive story. Instead during her sessions she would go into long monologues, belaboring unimportant details. The analyst sensed that the purpose of the patient's behavior was: (1) to offer entertainment, as though it were expected of her, and (2) to mock him, as though she were very slyly making a fool of him. He remembered her many statements that during visits home Frances felt obliged to entertain her grandmother, as she had done ever since she was a child. It occurred to him that her mockery might be hiding rage, and one day he asked her if she felt that she was lying on the couch for his entertainment, assuming that his more mature age made it necessary to entertain him as she did her grandmother. She told him that when she was 5 she had amused herself by making a stage with wooden blocks and having toy singers perform on it. "Of course, the blocks belonged to *him*," she explained. "Him?" he asked. "He" turned out to be her mother's younger and only brother, Francis. This was how the analyst learned about the dead pilot and afterward he began to consider Frances a replacement child with the task of "entertaining" the mourners, while indirectly expressing her rage against this impossible task.

As treatment progressed the analyst and the patient understood that her preoccupation with spirits, astral planes, reincarnation, and related topics had a great deal to do with her having been chosen as a "replacement child." In treatment, at one point, Frances reported that her mother's dead sibling "lived on the highest level" or astral plane. It seemed as though her grandmother's (and mother's) conscious fantasy that Francis' spirit arose from his coffin and went up to heaven (i.e., space) had been passed to the child who internalized it as a "psychic truth." The patient's expectations of "visits" from space aliens was in the service of her trying to integrate, in adulthood, her self representation with the object representation deposited in her, which she later externalized into space. Throughout her life this integration eluded her.

When she experienced the deposited representation within herself, her inability to integrate it would make her feel that she had two layers of skin. In front of a mirror she would pinch her face in order to put the "two skins" together, without success. Once she underwent facial plastic surgery to achieve this aim. The surgeon had no idea of the procedure's significance to his patient—he was responding to the patient's "rationalized" wish to alter and beautify her face. The psychodynamics of this surgery were similar to the psychodynamics of transsexuals who undergo surgery in order to establish a "fit" between their internal demands and their external appearance. Out of six persons studied by Volkan (1981, 1987) who carried unintegrated deposited representations of older siblings, two had the same symptom of thinking they had two layers of skin and having plastic surgery to fix it. Like all transsexuals, Frances was not successful in finding a solution to a psychological problem through surgical changes.

The Masque of the Red Death

Frances' favorite author was Edgar Allan Poe, that death-obsessed writer known to have faced early childhood loss with the death of his mother. Poe's tale, *The Masque of the Red Death*, was especially important to Frances. Not only did she know the details of this story, but its images would appear in her dreams. Poe's story tells of a prince and his followers hiding away in a castle to escape a pestilence that overtakes them in spite of their precautions and that makes blood spring from the pores of their faces. Such a story might suggest in a neurotic woman a perception of the "blood" of menstruation displaced to the face. Whether or not the story held such a meaning for her, the notion of the Red Death contributed to Frances' self-concept. In a dream about the Poe story she was in a castle, afflicted by the Red Death but with its characteristic disfigurement in only *half* of her face. She was wearing a sheetlike dress that reminded her of a hospital gown or a shroud—she was a ghost. Her associations related to Francis, whose face and body had been badly burned. Having the disfigurement in only one-half of her face once more was related to her inability to integrate her self-concept with the deposited representation: two different halves was another version of two layers of skin. The Red Death also stood for Frances' murderous rage which was partly formed from her mother's and grandmother's projections of their aggression into the adopted daughter.

The Night of the Living Dead

One time Frances described how she had felt when a spirit from space entered her body for the first time. She said it felt as though a cancer were eating her insides. The grandmother and the mother had idealized the representation of Francis, but they transmitted their ambivalence toward it too. Furthermore, for Frances the Francis/fetus representation would become "bad" whenever she projected her own aggression into this representation. Therefore, even though she initially perceived the spirit (the Francis/fetus representation) as "good" and digestible, by the time it entered her body it had become dangerous. She had to prevent it from remaining inside of her. As a defense against her incorporative and cannibalistic fantasies pertaining to taking in (identification with) the dreaded object representation, as an adult, Frances would not eat meat—she was a vegetarian. Even so, the cannibalistic fantasies would not disappear.

Night of the Living Dead is one of the most popular movies on American university campuses. It is a horror film in which the dead eat the living in order to live themselves. Young adult college students go to see this movie, which is often shown late at night at campus theaters. The students sometimes dress like the characters in the movie, and as the characters speak on the screen they join in the dialogue. We suspect that the increased postadolescent introjective—projective relatedness and search for new (more adult) identities and new objects make this movie popular with this group. One does not have to be psychotic to be temporarily "addicted" to this movie. However, in Frances the movie induced deep responses. As a teenager, she began to see the movie repeatedly. It always fascinated her; it was *not* frightening for her. For Frances the content of this movie was "familiar," it directly reflected her "eating up" a dead fetus and a dead man and her keeping them "alive" within herself or externalizing them in the spirits and constantly relating to them.

8 TWINNING

As in the situation of deposited representation described in the previous chapter, in a clinical condition called "twinning" a child is preoccupied with the representation of another sibling, but usually a living one. We apply the term *twinning* to a particular and pathological self and object relationship between siblings. This relationship manifests itself in interpersonal interactions, but we use the term to focus on intrapsychic processes with their associated unconscious fantasies.

On the interpersonal level we may notice the pairing of two siblings. The siblings may or may not be biological twins; biological twinship is not a necessary condition for twinning. The pair, however, speak of themselves as "twins" or "blood siblings." Sometimes they have ritually bonded themselves together by pricking their fingers and mixing their blood. The twinning siblings consider themselves as one functional unit. They may, for example, describe their relationship using the analogy of a "three-legged team" (such as one finds at children's outings and competitions) to describe how they function together. In childhood they exhibit a need for daily physical contact and closeness and they may engage in mutual masturbation. They usually share daydreams in which both are "actors" or "actresses" involved in joint adventures which result in their remaining a pair forever.

In our experience and in the experience of the colleagues with whom we consulted, twinning, as we describe it here, more often occurs between a sister and brother than between same-sexed siblings. In heterosexual twinning the children are consciously aware that they share one penis. In our view the third leg of the "three-legged team" stands for the shared penis; however, the children usually do not seem aware of this meaning. In their joint daydreams the pair will marry each other when they grow up. If the pair is not composed of biological twins but of siblings of different ages, one of them may go through the adolescent passage prior to the other one. As the older one becomes an adolescent, a "separation" often occurs between the two siblings. Then they will go their separate ways, but the memory of their twinning (and the psychological influence of it) never disappears.

As in the situation of deposited representations, the mother's or adult caregiver's conscious, but more importantly, unconscious fantasies play a role in the development of twinning between siblings. Such adult unconscious fantasies and conscious expressions of similar wishes often dovetail with the twinning children's unconscious fantasies and conscious expressions. The adults, for example, may arrange that the twinning children sleep in the same bed during their developmental years, wear the same kind of clothing, and so on.

From the point of view of the internal worlds of the twinning children we see a similarity between having "imaginary companions" (Freiberg, 1959; Nagera, 1969) and twinning in the sense that both the "imaginary companion" and the "twin" symbolically represent an externalized aspect of the child. If the child creates an imaginary companion to respond to her loneliness we say that the imaginary companion is a fantasized and wished-for object representation to fulfill her dependency needs. If she creates an imaginary companion as a reservoir for her envious self, for example, we say that the imaginary companion is an externalized "bad" self representation. There is, however, a major difference between an imaginary companion and a living person whom the child imagines is her "twin." The *reality* of the interactions between twinning children makes the internalization of their experiences a concrete factor which influences the structures of their internal worlds more than would the experience with an imaginary companion. The imaginary companion is under the absolute control of its creator, while a "twin" cannot be fully controlled—a "negotiation" with the other is required, making the twinning experience more complex.

In the situation of a deposited representation the child makes attempts to identify with what had been deposited in her. But identification is not usually a goal of the typical twinning situation. Instead, the aim of twinning is to make the representation of the sibling available for service at all times: the representation of the "twin" is utilized, whenever necessary, to patch up the child's own sense of self. Furthermore, the child's ego functions and responses to superego have to be shared with those that belong to the "twin." Once the "twins" are physically separated (i.e., in adulthood), they continue to utilize each other's self representations and associated ego functions to negotiate self and object relations issues and psychosexual or aggressive conflicts. The bond is forever! If this internalized twinning is threatened, the individual experiences anxiety and may develop symptoms to deal with the anxiety.

Sometimes a kind of twinning occurs between children who are not siblings, but who, at least in fantasy, share certain "fates" and use each other to patch up their senses of self. For example, Nickman (1985) refers to the case of Bill, a 14-year-old who formed a "pact" with a friend, not a sibling. "They were convinced that they were biological siblings because they were both adopted and had similar interests" (p. 375). The two youngsters rubbed each other's knuckles with sandpaper until they bled, and then they mixed their blood. Nickman notes that this was a repetitive behavior, a symbolic enactment of their "blood brotherhood" (p. 375).

Twins

Because the term *twinning* sounds like biological twinship, it might make sense to consider using another term in order not to confuse pathological intrapsychic self and object relationships with the relationships between actual twins. We prefer using the term *twinning*, however, because those involved in twinning, whether actual twins or not, usually refer to each other as twins, they consider their behavior patterns the outcome of being actual twins, and they often have a fantasy of sharing the same blood (blood brotherhood or sisterhood). Thus, the pathological state of twinning is connected with the concept of actual twinship and so an examination of the literature on actual twins will be useful to us here.

In the general psychological literature there are a great many papers on the psychology of twins, basically exploring the question of nature versus nurture. Because of their genetic makeup, twins provide a real opportunity for examining genetic variables in human development. One often finds references to twin studies in works that attempt to answer the question: What is most important in a child's development—biological–genetic factors or environment?

In the psychoanalytic literature, too, papers dealing with the psychology of twins, though not particularly with twinnings, are abundant. Many of them concern the possible "vulnerability" in twins pertaining to such issues as individuation, self-image, and identity (Burlingham, 1952); ego differentiation (Lidz, Schafer, Fleck, Cornelison, and Terry, 1962); parental perception (Allen, Greenspan, and Pollin, 1976); and interplay between biological factors and early experience (Dibble and Cohen, 1980; 1981). Psychoanalysts have also studied "normal" personality development in twins. For example, Dibble and Cohen (1981) discussed parental influence on twins' psychology. They conducted a longitudinal study of over fifty sets of twins and their families. They write:

> Even before their birth, the children in the twinship were seen as having or lacking individuality, and as having the capacity to provide pleasure or deprive their parents of it. The twins, perhaps more than singletons, were the object of fantasy and were members of the family long before they entered the world. Some parents of twins were more interested in the rarity of being parents of twins and were excited by the attention the twins brought; others were concerned about how to individualize the children and yet treat them equally. Some worried about whether they would have enough love for both children; others about the competitiveness

that the children would experience with each other; still other parents believed that the children would be lifelong companions for one another, helping each other through crises and always being available for support [pp. 64-65].

Other psychoanalytic writers (Joseph, 1959; Arlow, 1960; Glenn, 1974; Hamilton, 1995) on the psychology of actual twinship list clinical findings such as intense rivalry or strong ties, the fantasy of being only half a person, the protracted identification of one twin with the other, and so on. These writers do not necessarily differentiate the psychology of actual twinship from pathological twinning as we describe it here. It appears that in some twins they noted characteristics of twinning; that is, difficulty in differentiating self and object representations and utilizing the other's representation to patch up one's own sense of self, attempts to share ego functions—and listed them as natural aspects of the psychology of twinship. We think that in spite of certain similarities, the pathological condition of twinning should be differentiated from the normal psychology of twinship. One of us, Volkan, has analyzed two twins, one identical and one nonidentical, and pathological twinning did not exist in either of them.

Ainslie (1985) studied a total of twenty-six sets of twins. The group represented different twinships (i.e., fraternal or identical), and their ages ranged from 14 to 72. Ainslie was interested in understanding the "environmental side" of the psychology of twins. He discovered that while it may be accurate to speak of a specific psychology of twinship, twins are not fundamentally different from nontwins. "Although the specific conditions of twin development lend themselves to specific characteristics of personality organization, nontwins raised under similar circumstances, for example, siblings who are quite close in age, may very closely resemble twins psychologically" (p. xi). It is beyond the scope of this book to review completely and critically all of the literature on the psychology of twins. Rather, keeping in mind that our focus is on the sibling representation in adults' minds, we will explore the phenomenon of twinning as an internal process as it appears in adulthood.

While the fate of the related concept, deposited representation, does not lead to pathology in adulthood in every case, we think that the consequences of twinning, as we describe it here, persist into adulthood and do lead to psychopathology. In instances of deposited representations, pathology occurs—as it did in the case of Frances (see previous chapter)—if the individual cannot adapt internally to the representation which has been deposited in her self representation. The nonintegration between the child's self representation and the deposited representation always causes trouble for the adult, unless the child successfully integrates it and lives up to the idealization of the deposited representation—then it may in fact enrich the child's ego functions, self-esteem, and repertoire of behavior patterns. In contrast, twinning in childhood means that no integration has taken place between the representation of the child and the representation of her sibling with whom she is twinning. Identifications in twinning are temporary since there is more emphasis on holding onto the "twin's" representation for patching up one's identity. In twinning the other's representation can make or break the first individual's psychic structure.

A WOMAN WITH A "WORRY STONE"

A middle-aged woman, Mary, a college graduate and mother of three children, became Dr. William Greer's patient; she was suffering from depressive episodes and drinking spells. Mary's father, a tavern owner and an alcoholic, was the father of five young children when his first wife died. He married Mary's mother, also an alcoholic, and they had five children. When Mary was born she was her father's ninth child. Mary had a brother, Donovan, a year older than she. When she was 9 years old her mother delivered a baby girl, the last child in the family.

At the beginning of the second year of treatment Mary told Dr. Greer that she had withheld a "significant historical fact I have known to be vital in my developmental saga." With the solemnity of a confessional (Mary is Catholic), she disclosed that her one-year-older brother Donovan, was, in truth, a fraternal twin born just before she. While she felt bad about her breach of honesty, she nonetheless felt justified in it inasmuch as she thought that Dr. Greer might misjudge the importance of this

information: "You would have made just far too much out of it."
Dr. Greer and his consultant, Dr. Volkan, were puzzled by this.
At first they believed that Mary and Donovan were fraternal twins.
It took them some time to realize that the patient's initial history
about Donovan being a year older was the "historical truth."
During her therapeutic regression, in the beginning of the second year of her treatment, Mary in her sessions began exhibiting
her "psychic truth"—that she and her brother were twins. Then,
for one-and-one-half years on the couch, Mary spoke of her "fraternal twin" and reenacted her "childhood world" until she finally returned to reality and referred to Donovan as a year-older
brother. During this one-and-one-half year period she exhibited
many aspects of twinning with Donovan's mental representation.

Childhood

Mary's early environmental conditions and her mother were influential in Mary's twinning with Donovan. Before Mary's birth
her parents' home was not a happy one. The father would come
home drunk, threaten his wife and his children, and exhibit rage
and violence. Mary's mother was overwhelmed by the responsibili-
ties of caring for so many children, and she withdrew from them.
She did not plan to have Mary. When Mary was born her mother
put her in Donovan's bed as if she were an extension of him, as
if Mary had never been born. The two children, from Mary's early
life on, slept together. Later their mother gave them the same
toys and dressed them in identical clothes. The children grew up
masturbating each other every night. In addition, Mary recalled
feeling responsible for Donovan, since she thought he was the
more fragile one.

When Mary was 6 years old Donovan pricked their fingers
and mixed their blood in order to be "one" and they made a
pact that they would be in love forever. They spoke of marrying
each other when they grew up, and they selected aristocratic
names for their children (in fact, Donovan, as an adult gave these
names to his children). If they were forced to marry others, they
would wait until their spouses died and then they would marry
each other. They would be, as Mary recalled, "united in an eter-
nal state of beatitude from which the rest of the world would be

excluded." It would just be the two of them, "now, always, and forever." One can hear echoes of the Catholic liturgy in her words.

When Mary was 8 and Donovan 9 years old their parents, thinking that the children were too old now to sleep together, separated their beds. Mary and Donovan were enraged. Mary recalled screaming obscenities at her parents and God and wishing to be dead because of the separation. From this time on there was no physical closeness with Donovan, but mental closeness to his representation and twinning as a mental phenomenon remained in Mary's mind.

Mary's rage about the physical separation from her "twin" was mainly directed to her baby sister, who was born the year of this separation. In Mary's fantasy the "intruder" had caused this separation and she feared that the baby would replace Mary by twinning with Donovan. Once Mary was left alone with her baby sister on a balcony. The baby was in a baby buggy. Mary pushed the buggy off the balcony, but it fell on some shrubs and the baby was unharmed. The adults thought of this incident as an accident, but Mary (like Mira in chapter 6), knew that she had attempted to murder her little sister. As an adult Mary would periodically entertain murderous thoughts about this sister.

Adulthood

Their being separated also heightened Mary's resolve to identify with her brother. If they were not physically together she could keep him within her by becoming like him. She became a "tomboy" and began to dress like a boy. She also would go off into the woods, where, assured that she could not be heard, she would scream obscenities at God for not making her a boy. She felt inferior as a girl and was preoccupied with thoughts of having bodily deformities. Her nose was too long or her feet were too large or her breasts were too bulbous. She was ashamed of these "deformities" and she made every effort to camouflage them. Like transsexuals do, she felt that nature had played a trick on her and imprisoned her in the body of the wrong sex. She had conscious fantasies of a penis sewn onto her genitalia. She became a regular at her father's tavern—just one of the young men! After a priest seduced her she became a prostitute and thus "collected" penises. In her late teens she married one of her customers, a rigid, moral, and inhibiting figure, whom she used as an external superego. Now Mary became a woman with high morals. After a time she gave birth to fraternal twins, but the male child died within hours of his birth. In her treatment Dr. Greer learned how this event became condensed in Mary's mind with the physical separation from Donovan at the age of 8. Two years after having the twins, she had a boy, for whom "no sacrifice was too great." Soon her husband, like both of her parents, became an alcoholic, and during one of their fights he shot at her with a pistol, but missed. They were divorced. Mary, with her father's financial help, rented an apartment, moved there with her two children, went to see a psychiatrist, and started to attend college. There she met a handsome man and married him. This marriage lasted only six months. But while she was married to this man, Mary once more became pregnant, and had a miscarriage. Mary felt she was responsible for "murdering" this baby; as a response she became religious and more moralistic. She called her first husband who meanwhile had stopped drinking and became religious. Once more they were married and they stayed together.

As she embarked upon her remarriage to her first husband, Mary heard of a baby, a girl, who was abandoned by her mother and was living in the custody of her biological father. She developed a thought: I have to have this baby. She manipulated the adoption system and managed to take the baby home. For the next 13 years she was involved in a legal battle with the biological father of this baby until she won and legally adopted the child: "I would have killed him [the baby's biological father] for this baby," Mary once told Dr. Greer.

During the legal battle Mary had stopped her college education. After the battle was over she went back to college, received a professional degree, and began working in her profession. Meanwhile Donovan, who had been living in another state and having little contact with Mary, was divorced from his wife. Soon after that he met another woman and without informing Mary, he married for the second time. This bothered Mary tremendously. It should be recalled that during her childhood she and

Donovan had made a pact: if both were forced to marry other persons and if their spouses died, they would then marry each other. In spite of the fact that Mary was divorced twice and married three times, she perceived Donovan's recent divorce and remarriage as a "betrayal." When her brother remarried, she lost her "twin" again. After this event Mary began having depressive episodes and drinking spells. These are the symptoms which eventually led her to seek help. At first she became a patient of a psychiatrist who "stepped right into the shoes of my brother." When this therapist moved to a new location Mary once more lost her "twin" brother. The therapist was not psychoanalytically oriented and he never discussed Mary's transference to him in which she made him like her "twin." After leaving this treatment she came to see Dr. Greer, at the peak of an unresolved transference neurosis toward her previous therapist.

Magical Inanimate Objects

The above summary of this patient's history suggests that many factors, conscious and unconscious, contributed to Mary's psychopathology. In order to be able to focus on the twinning issue and its condensation with other key factors, we now turn our attention to Mary's magical inanimate objects.

As Dr. Greer slowly learned Mary's history, he realized that her unresolved transference toward her previous therapist was now directed to him. He was the "twin" brother. Separation from him (e.g., due to canceled hours), was traumatic. But Dr. Greer also noticed something else. Mary was also afraid that "closeness" to the representation of Donovan would induce a sense of "suffocation" in her. On several occasions, when she felt "suffocated" on Dr. Greer's couch Mary would request that her therapist's door be left ajar so that she might escape if need be. At such times we can say that Mary was claustrophobic and that Dr. Greer's office was a womb containing "twins." Her wishing *and* dreading to fuse the representation of herself with that of Donovan/Dr. Greer had to be controlled and balanced. Mary had symbolically controlled this balancing act through the utilization of a magical inanimate object: a small piece of polished stone. She

called it her "worry stone." The existence of this stone was initially Mary's secret. After Mary plunged into a therapeutic regression and declared that Donovan was her fraternal twin, and she
began recreating her psychic truth regarding twinning on the
couch, one day she told Dr. Greer about her "worry stone." She
opened her hand to reveal a polished stone wrapped in tissue.
She then disclosed that, since the inception of her treatment, she
never came to her sessions without it. It had been her routine
since childhood to keep a "worry stone" on her person as a kind
of amulet.

We would like to digress here from Mary's case and explore
briefly the magical inanimate objects which patients secretly bring
to their sessions. Volkan (1976) first reported on such phenomena when he described the case of Margaret, a case that also
illustrates twinning. Margaret's mother was a twin and Margaret
was conceived during an interval in which her mother was for a
time living far away from her twin sister and feeling "incomplete"
without her. Subsequently Margaret's four siblings—two older
and two younger than she—paired off, leaving Margaret paired
with her mother. Volkan wrote "They were so close that when
Margaret was ill they often rested side by side on the bed with
their bodies curved reciprocally together as though they were the
halves of a fused whole" (p. 227).

A behavioral peculiarity Margaret adopted in childhood and
continued into adult life with a kind of addiction, was her habit
of collecting bits of lint and rolling them between her fingers
into "fuzz balls." Margaret secretly brought these "fuzz balls"
to her analytic sessions. Volkan (1976) gives the details of his
understanding of the meaning of Margaret's magical inanimate
objects. Margaret's self and object representations might fuse in
her relationships with significant others in *intimate* situations.
However, she was able to differentiate between her self representation and object representations in other relationships. In her
intimate relationship with her analyst the "fuzz balls" were in
the service of controlling her fusing and differentiation from Dr.
Volkan's representation. The "fuzz balls" included elements of
reactivated transitional objects. They also included fetishistic
qualities. Likewise, Mary's "worry stone" had condensed multiple
meanings. Returning to Mary's case, we will explore the role of

the "worry stone" as a defense against fusing her representation with the representation of Donovan/Dr. Greer. Furthermore, we will show that this magical inanimate object also served other functions.

During the period when Mary called Donovan her fraternal twin in her sessions, she talked about him constantly. She reported sharing her thoughts and plans with him. In fact, she had not seen Donovan, who lived in another state, for years. They had little communication. However, whenever her telephone rang, Mary expected it to be her brother calling. Along with talking about Donovan, Mary also talked about her magical inanimate objects.

When Mary disclosed the existence of her "worry stone" her associations were to a doll that she slept with as a latency-aged child. She recognized in retrospect that this doll was a substitute for the brother with whom she shared a bed until she was 8 years old. On the back of the doll was a zippered pocket in which she hid stones she collected, as well as candy. During her childhood, nobody was permitted to touch this doll except Mary and Donovan. Mary slept with her head on the doll, feeling the solid objects in the zippered pocket. She confided that this same doll occupied an obligatory portion of her current conjugal bed. She then connected a symptom (somnambulism) that had occurred on the first night of her honeymoon (the second marriage to her present husband) with the absence of the doll.

Mary's associations to the doll revealed multiple meanings. She was sure that the doll had become a prominent object for her after she was physically separated from Donovan. However, she also thought that it might have existed even when they were sharing the same bed. Recalling her two opposing feelings about Dr. Greer—anxiety over being separated from him and fear of suffocation when she was with him—Mary was able to understand that like the polished stone she brought to her sessions, the doll was a kind of buffer, under her absolute control: it helped her to balance the wish for and the dread of merging with Donovan and his representation. Mary would feel the hardness of stones or candy within the doll when she put her head on it. Taking into consideration the poor mothering Mary received, we wondered if the pressure of the solid parts of the doll on Mary's head gave her a needed sense of "boundary" so that she could go to sleep. In this sense the "hardness" of the doll stood for a "containing" mother. Mary also was consciously aware of the doll representing Donovan with its "hardness" representing his penis. When describing this awareness Mary extolled the virtues of being a "twin." "As a twin," she said, "I never had to compete for attention because I had a twin to run to." "I'm one up on you, Dr. Greer," she smugly added, "because I have something that neither you nor anyone else can ever take away from me." When Mary separated from Donovan she felt "damaged" unless she "stole" his penis.

When her therapist canceled a session during this period of her treatment Mary had an impulse to "steal" solid items from a store. (Margaret, too, had a symptom of stealing solid objects.) Then, in a dream Mary saw blood on her therapist's arm. Her associations showed that the blood represented a separation from Donovan/Dr. Greer, and it also represented her wish to kill her brother (and now the therapist) in order to steal the penis.

In one of her sessions Mary asked: "To whom does the penis belong?" She recalled a horse her father owned whose size was awesome to her as a child. She loved to ride the horse but "I could never stay in the saddle" (i.e., she could not control owning a penis [horse] between her legs). "Donovan," she said "could mount and ride that horse without any assistance so I made myself into a man [in order] not to be envious of him." Mary began to laugh as she recalled a dream from the previous night in which she had a four-inch-long growth of hair on her arms; if the horse could not be between her legs, she could at least grow long hair (penis).

Condensed Meanings of the "Worry Stone"

Speaking of her "worry stone," Mary declared: "It's my security blanket." She described it as necessary for soothing her anxiety and keeping "bad spirits" away. In this description it sounds as though the stone functioned as a transitional object. But it was also a "childhood fetish" (Sperling, 1963; Dickes, 1978) or "psychotic fetish" (Mahler, 1968). "Childhood fetish" refers to an inanimate object used when there are disturbances in early object relations. Its function is to deal with the separation anxiety of key developmental phases: at weaning, when the mother's breast is given up; at the anal phase, when the feces is given up; or at the oedipal phase, when the parent of the opposite sex is given up. The childhood fetish can be reactivated in adult life when the individual senses a need to respond to preoedipal conflicts.

Mahler's concept of the "childhood psychotic fetish" resembles the views of Sperling and Dickes on "childhood fetishes." It deals with early separation–individuation issues. Unlike the typical transitional object, it is not a soft object (e.g., a blanket), or a part of the child's own body (e.g., hair), or a magical toy (e.g., a teddy bear); it is usually a cold and hard object, such as a fan, a jar, or, as in Mary's case, a stone. In her doll (soft) with a stone (hard) in it Mary most likely had combined transitional object characteristics with childhood psychotic fetish characteristics.

The original "worry stone" was given to her by her parish priest when she was 6 years old. It was a polished piece of bone. In fact, Mary still had this original inanimate object—she kept it in a bank vault, even after it lost its magic during her treatment with Dr. Greer. What she brought to her treatment was not this piece of bone, but a polished piece of stone which in Mary's mind was connected with or stood for the bone in the bank vault.

The examination of the priest's "gift" illustrated how Donovan's penis was also condensed with Mary's father's penis, as we will describe shortly. Now Mary "owned" both penises, since the bone represented them both. She kept the bone locked up so that it could not be stolen from her. Here the inanimate object was much like a classic "fetish" described by Freud (1927); this fetish stood for a penis without which its owner would feel castrated.

Since Mary was raised as a Catholic, most likely the priest's gift also had religious significance for her. It reflected a form of redemption. She held it like one holds a rosary to do penance. By locking up the piece of bone she could "own" the penis, but also not feel guilty for stealing it.

The Father's Detachable Eye-Penis

The story of the piece of bone belonged to a period when Mary's father's had a near-fatal automobile accident; Mary was 6 years old. Soon after this accident Mary's father's left eye, pierced by a shard of glass, had to be removed. He was fitted with a glass eye. This was a very stressful year for the family. During the course of this year Mary's father slowly recuperated from his injuries. With sadistic pleasure, he would take out his glass eye in front of his children. Mary and Donovan were horrified at the sight of the empty socket. They came to believe that because that eye never closed when he slept, the eye (as a harsh superego) could watch their every move. Mary vividly recalled a conscious fantasy she had whenever she saw the glass eye in a vial he used to soak it. In this fantasy she would snatch the eye and hide it where it could never be found.

Mary could not recall if the piece of bone was given to her before or after her father's accident. However, she was sure that it was given to her that particular stressful year. No matter what the timing was, in her treatment Mary understood how she had made her bone/"worry stone" represent Donovan's as well as her father's "detachable" penis.

In the transference she became afraid of looking at Dr. Greer "in the eye." She said that he looked "shifty" to her and this made her anxious. Her anxiety steadily escalated as the wish to appropriate the detachable eye/penis was displaced into transference. Now the patient wished to flee treatment to avoid fantasized reprisal by her therapist. In a dream a person whose name included a variation of the word *penis* in it came to visit the patient. In a second dream from the same night, Mary was lost in a hotel. She entered a bathroom and stole toilet tissue (it should be recalled that when she first showed her "worry stone" to Dr. Greer it was wrapped in tissue. The penis was also connected with feces. For our purpose here we do not discuss her separation anxieties at the anal level.) Her therapist explained that Mary's father's glass eye symbolized a detachable penis—condensed with Donovan's penis—over which she competed for ownership. If she triumphed in the competition for this coveted organ, as she did in her dreams, she would have to flee lest she be castrated (i.e., an "eye for an eye"). Once she understood her wish to escape from having to face the source of her anxiety, Mary gave up the idea of leaving treatment. She also understood the condensation between Donovan, her father, and also her lost baby (a twin who only lived a few hours), and her obsession to "steal" her adopted child to replace her losses. Toward the end of the third year of her treatment her "worry stone" began to lose its magic and Mary no longer brought it to her sessions.

Intrapsychic Separation from her "Twin"

Gradually Mary was out of her "deep" regression and now she was "reconstructing" her childhood twinning while on the couch. She had managed to get Donovan to send her some old photographs taken of them (Mary and Donovan) as children. The therapist sensed that by examining these pictures Mary was testing the reality that Donovan was indeed one year older than her. Her attempts at separating from her "twin" induced fantasies of killing her brother. This feeling was so strong that every time the telephone rang she became alarmed that she would hear the news of her brother's—or a friend's—death. For two weeks in a quasi-delusional state she awaited the arrival of the police to arrest her for murder! She developed compulsive symptoms such as checking and rechecking the gas stove to be certain that she had not forgotten to turn it off. She was concerned with the safety of others as well as herself. At work she was afraid that she might accidentally kill her coworkers. Then, Mary spontaneously linked her symptoms with the therapeutic work on her intrapsychic relationship with Donovan and the twinning. She stated that "This separation thing leaves me with no purpose. We were like a couple with three legs. Together we were hermaphroditic—both male and female." It was as if life without this brother and the penis they shared was inconceivable. She could neither live with him nor without him. After this period of her treatment Mary once more told Dr. Greer that her brother Donovan was a year older and she stopped speaking of him as a fraternal twin.

Mary's mother had died before Mary came to see Dr. Greer. But her father died after Mary had done a great deal of work in her treatment and had gone through intrapsychic separation from the representation of Donovan. The father first suffered a cerebral hemorrhage that rendered him comatose. He was in a hospital for over a month before he died. The father's hospitalization and death brought Mary and Donovan together since they both visited their father during this time. As Mary and Donovan stood vigil by the father's bed she noticed that his glass eye would not stay in his socket due to increased intracranial pressure. "It just kept popping out," she said. That the eye would not stay in induced anxiety in her which she dealt with by trying to force the extruded eye back into place. She persisted in this until a nurse advised Mary to just remove it. With trepidation she discontinued her futile efforts. After his death, however, she made certain that it was "in his head where it belonged."

The father's death mobilized grief over losing an oedipal father and brought back memories of father as a caring person when not drunk. In a dream Mary angrily told her mother that she no longer intended to care for a little boy she assumed to be her "twin" brother. The mother told her that Mary could excuse herself from this duty under the condition that she marry a Catholic priest well known to the family. Her associations to this dream indicated that the priest was her father and that if she did not "twin" with Donovan and became a "woman," she would have "normal" oedipal strivings pertaining to a father figure. In the dream Mary had a strong sexual desire for the priest. She recalled her father's objections to all of the boys she dated. "My father acted more like a jealous lover than a father," she added.

Recalling her attempts to be a "tomboy" and drinking in her father's tavern, Mary was pleased that she had given up, in the last year of treatment, "drowning myself in alcohol."

After her father's death Mary developed a new symptom and Dr. Greer felt that it reflected progress in her psychic growth. The symptom was itching and scratching at night in bed. Elbirlik (1980) and Volkan (1987) have written about this symptom as an attempt on the part of patients to establish psychological borders between them and others by "separating the skin of one from that of the other" (Volkan, 1987, p. 142). Dr. Greer made a similar interpretation regarding Mary's itching. A week after this her symptom resolved itself, and some months later Mary's treatment ended.

9 DEAD SIBLING REPRESENTATIONS

Twinning with a sibling's representation may continue even after the "twin" sibling dies. To illustrate this, in the next chapter we will describe the internal world of a woman, Gisela, in her early forties. Her case exhibits many aspects of an adult's unconscious sibling experience initiated by the death of a sibling. Before giving details of Gisela's internal world, however, we focus on aspects of internal responses to losing a sibling, whether the sibling is older or younger. The question we want to answer is this: What does an adult do with the representation of a sibling who dies during the former's childhood and what kind of psychopathology may result from internal interactions with such a representation?

Observable reactions of children to the death of an important other, including a sibling, have been published abundantly in the psychoanalytic, psychiatric, and psychological literature. Since these findings are commonly known by the clinical practitioner and are too extensive to summarize here, we have decided not to make a list of them. Instead, we will discuss the metapsychology of childhood mourning and focus on the fate of the mental representation in an adult's mind of a dead sibling by providing the case of Carol.

CHILDHOOD MOURNING

There is some controversy among psychoanalysts as to when a child is capable of mourning. Bowlby (1960, 1969) emphasized in his "attachment theory" that mourning is possible in infancy, a view that has been widely criticized, most notably by Anna Freud (1960), among others. She stated that the process of mourning includes the individual's effort to accept a change in the external world (the loss of the cathected object) and to effect corresponding changes in the inner world (withdrawal of libido from the lost object, identification with the lost object, and so on). She went on to reason that the term *mourning*—an intrapsychic process—should not be applied to the separation reactions of infants. Separation reactions, metapsychologically speaking, are not identical with mourning.

To say that an infant or a very young child can mourn, we would have to show that he possesses a mental ability which can differentiate self and object representations, test reality, accept the reality principle, and control, at least partially, id tendencies such as murderous rage toward the dead object (since by dying the object causes a narcissistic injury in the mourner). These capacities are still undeveloped in the infant according to most evidence, even though the recent research (i.e., Emde, 1988a,b; Dowling and Rothstein, 1989; Greenspan, 1989) indicates more potential for various ego functions in the infant and very small child than we previously thought. Therefore, we still agree with Anna Freud that we cannot apply the term *mourning* to the separation reactions of the infant, because, while active, the mind of an infant is not capable of mourning.

Object constancy is a key concept in child development (Hartmann, 1952; A. Freud, 1965; Mahler, 1968). Prior to the development of object constancy, that is, prior to the development of the child's ability to integrate and maintain internally representations of the other, such as mother, even when the other is not present, the pleasure–pain principle governs the child's response to a loss. Loss, for example, may be experienced as a sense similar to hunger. Thus, in considering mourning in children the child's chronological age is crucial. The more the child is able to maintain object constancy, as well as self constancy (Settlage, 1991), the closer his or her mourning will resemble an adult's. Furman (1964) stated that, in general, it is not until a child is between 3 1/2 and 4 years of age that he can mourn, and Wolfstein (1969) hypothesized that passage through adolescence is a necessary condition for the ability to mourn *genuinely*—as an adult mourns and as Freud (1917a) described it.

During the adolescent passage there occurs an obligatory psychobiological regression, and what Blos (1979) calls a "second individuation." This obligatory regression causes the youngster to revisit preoedipal as well as oedipal relationships and "relive" them. As the youngster decathects from, or at least modifies, his childhood object representations, he becomes involved in new identifications (with "the friend," "the group," etc.). In other words, during the adolescent passage there is a "letting go" or changing of existing object representations while forming new ones, and then even identifying with them. This obligatory psychological passage resembles Freud's description of mourning in that important representations are scrutinized, reevaluated, and put into a new, revised context. Successfully traversing a "normal" adolescent passage will give the individual the ability to experience an adult-type mourning process and will allow him to mourn over losses in the future as would an adult.

Significant object loss during the developmental years can have drastic consequences. No wonder that, as the developing child or youngster attempts to adapt to the loss externally, and more importantly, internally, some difficulties will be handled by the formation of unconscious fantasies. The fantasies might include the representation of the loss or lost person, often with multiple meanings. These unconscious fantasies will be influenced by the developmental tasks of the child at the time of the occurrence of the loss and by the parents' conscious or unconscious thoughts about the loss which are passed to the child. In turn the child's unconscious fantasies later may play crucial roles in the nature of the individual's adult behavior patterns, character traits, or symptoms.

Berman (1978) describes sibling loss in childhood as an organizer of unconscious guilt and character pathology. As he indicates, however, not all adult reactions to death and losing a

significant other (including a sibling) result in pathological influences on the adult. Some childhood losses have outcomes
which reflect the mourner's utilization of sublimations and which
are considered valuable socially as well as by the individual. For
example, Abraham (1911) concluded that Segantini's paintings
reflected his reaction to the death of his mother when he was 5
years old. Since then many such "positive" outcomes have been
examined; for example, see Volkan (1981), Pollock (1989), Volkan and Zintl (1993).

Freud himself had personal experience with the positive consequences in adulthood of sibling loss in childhood. His brother
Julius died when Freud was 19 months old. His brother's death
caused a disruption in his relationship with his mother and nursemaid. Pollock (1989) and Rudnytsky (1988) believe that Freud's
childhood loss may have been a significant factor in the nature
of his creativity. In a work on Goethe, Freud (1917b) mentioned
Goethe's childhood belief that destiny had preserved his life although it had removed his brother (and grandmother). Thus,
Goethe believed that he was "a child of fortune" (p. 156). Since
Goethe no longer had to share his mother's love with a brother,
he became her unchallenged darling. Freud commented that "if
a man has been his mother's undisputed darling he retains
throughout life the triumphant feeling, the confidence in success,
which not seldom brings actual success along with it" (p. 156).

Hamilton (1976) postulates that in writing about Goethe's
experience, Freud also referred to himself and the derivatives of
Julius' death in Freud's own unconscious. Hamilton also suggests
that superstition in the adult Freud might have derived from his
unconscious childhood sibling experience. Hamilton reminds us
that in 1907 Freud said that even among educated people the
belief in spirits and ghosts do not disappear. Freud described how
a physician (probably himself) mistook the sister of a patient who
had died for the patient herself, and had momentarily thought:
"it's time that the dead can come back to life" (p. 71). He felt
shame when he realized his error.

We do not think that losing a sibling causes reactions different from those due to losing other significant people, such as a
parent. The key issue for our purpose here is how the representation of the dead sibling becomes symbolized and contaminated

with unconscious fantasies in the adult's mind. In the following case a young woman's loss of her brother resulted in a representation of the dead sibling contaminated with the representation of a penis.

A LOST BROTHER AS A LOST PENIS

Carol was a 24-year-old unmarried elementary school teacher who sought treatment three years after the death of one of her brothers in an automobile accident. Her psychoanalytic therapy was supervised, and the details of her case reported by Dr. Volkan (1981). She came to treatment because she was afraid that her relationship with her boyfriend would "die." She had feelings of inferiority and considered herself "damaged." While she had had such attitudes about herself in her earlier years she was aware that they had increased steadily since the death of her brother, Kenny.

She was conscious of her preoccupation with Kenny's images. In her room, for the last three years, she kept a picture of him between two candles, as though on an altar. She had adopted the habit of listening to records that were copies of those her brother had owned, which she had bought immediately after his death. She sometimes felt that he might come back from his grave or that other cherished friends or relatives might die suddenly.

Carol was the fourth of ten siblings. Her brother Kenny was born when she was 2 years old and he slept in the same room with her until she was 4 years old. During this time the siblings developed a special bond. Carol also envied him. As a child, she was very concerned with the anatomical differences between her and her brother. Closeness to Kenny played a role in her developing an unconscious fantasy that she once had a penis and that now it was lost.

In her small bedroom, among two siblings there was only one penis, and at times Carol did not "know" to whom it belonged. However, reality kept reminding her that the penis was between her brother's legs. When she was 4 years old she urinated in the bathroom in the presence of both her parents. Her father suddenly squatted before the toilet and, watching Carol's urination, commented that the urine seemed to be coming out of the "wrong hole." This event led to Carol's feeling that something was wrong with her genitals and that she was indeed "damaged." In turn, this increased both her investment in Kenny and his penis and her envy and sadism toward him.

At age 5 Kenny, and of course, his (her) penis was taken away from her when the two siblings were put in two different bedrooms. That year a male stranger touched Carol's genitals at a beach. Later in the same year a retarded neighbor boy took her into the woods, pulled down her panties, and like her father had done earlier, looked at her genitals. She wondered for a long time if these episodes had in some way "damaged" her.

Later Carol became the "skinniest" girl in the family. In her treatment it became evident that her "skinniness" was achieved in an attempt to provide a phallus—one now generalized to her whole body since the skinny and erect body symbolized the phallus. But such unconscious maneuvers obviously would be opposed by the reality principle. Furthermore, while she made her body a phallus, she also remained afraid of being castrated. After an elementary school teacher told a story about the devil pulling a sleeping woman's hair, Carol developed a protective ritual, which she maintained into adulthood, of bringing her hair (which also stood for a phallus) forward and holding onto it while she slept. She also began worrying at this time about part of her body dropping off if it protruded over the edge of her bed. Carol remained skinny throughout her teenage years.

Carol had sex for the first time at the age of 16. Soon her relationship with her sex partner ended and she drew very close to her brother Kenny. He consoled her about her loss, and the two spent much time together, talking and listening to records in his room. At the same time she began having dreams from which she would awaken with an orgasm but with no memory of the dream's content. She called her dreams "masturbation dreams" and was very concerned with the possibility that Kenny might have seen her dreaming and having an orgasm. In her treatment she became aware that at this period of her life she was "reactivating" her early childhood relationship with Kenny. He still had "their" penis. Her envy of him caused a reaction formation and an upsurge of sexual feelings for him. During her treatment she understood, through associations to her blank dreams, the reason why she could not remember the content of her dreams—they referred to her having sex with her sibling, sharing his (their) penis. When she was 19, her incestual urges toward Kenny made her so uncomfortable that she had to embark on a new relationship with a new boyfriend. At the age of 20, now disliking and disapproving of Kenny, she impulsively moved to a nearby city with her new boyfriend. Very shortly after making this move she learned of Kenny's sudden death in a car accident.

In Treatment

Selected aspects from Carol's treatment illustrate what she had done with the representation of her dead brother and how this representation was contaminated with her unconscious fantasy of obtaining his penis for herself. Very early in her treatment Carol's therapist was impressed with two observations:

1. Carol had identified with her brother (i.e., she had transient "beliefs" that now she bore a striking resemblance to him). Initially in her sessions she was dressed in a masculine mode of dress. She was also concerned about her legs being too hairy. It became obvious that she was recreating a phallus (with her body and dress) as well as "reincarnating" Kenny within herself.

2. She unconsciously believed that she (her envy) had killed him so that she could have "their" penis. In her first dream in the treatment there was a murder and she was being chased by someone (the therapist?) who wanted information from her about the murder.

Three months into her treatment Carol dreamed of driving on a country road while another car approached from the opposite direction. It was a convertible full of teenage boys, and as it passed, one of the boys was thrown out. Carol felt the force of the blow as he hit the ground and rolled over several times. As the boy struggled to get up, another car hit him head-on with terrible force. The boy was thrown to the edge of a cliff where he hung with his fingers until a steamroller came and crushed his hands, causing him to fall.

The discussion of this dream in treatment was very uncomfortable for Carol. In reality her brother had been riding on the passenger side of a car when another car had collided with it on that side. The force of the collision had hurled him out of the car and onto the road yards away. He had died later during emergency surgery.

What impressed us was that as the "author" of her dream, Carol again and again attempted to kill her brother—having another car hit him and a steamroller crush him (overdetermination)—as a reflection of her sadism against Kenny even while she identified with him, feeling the force of the blow as the boy hit the road. Sensing her aggression toward her brother, identification with him resulted in increasing Carol's feelings of being damaged. As a response to sensing her aggression Carol began to utilize avoidance mechanisms. She refused to watch any form of violence on television or in movies, and she avoided reading newspaper reports of violent occurrences. Through avoidance, unconsciously she was attempting not to recognize her own aggression and not to acknowledge the loss of her brother/penis. Therapeutic work slowly allowed her to recall and report the stories of her childhood, described earlier, when her feeling of being "damaged" and "inferior" had started. The brother was "superior" since "their" penis was between his legs. Carol even recalled visions of her brother in diapers. The mother would change Kenny's diapers in the bedroom she shared with her brother, and even that early in her life she was fascinated with Kenny's penis.

When Carol saw her therapist driving a car one day it stimulated her to displace her fantasies about Kenny onto her therapist. She, as a woman felt inferior while the therapist, as a man, she perceived as superior. But, since he was driving a car, he could be killed, too. In turn, she dreamed of climbing a ladder (penis) and of falling from it when the rung broke away beneath her feet (castration). Even if she killed Kenny or the therapist and regained the penis (the ladder), she was doomed to be castrated and lose her penis!

Carol informed her therapist that she had become pregnant. Her associations indicated that the fetus was a penis in her belly. She was afraid that her therapist would be angry and envious of her. The next month she menstruated—she was not pregnant after all. The loss of "the fetus" induced in her a sense that a part of her was missing. She now recalled that as soon as she heard of her brother's death she had had an identical feeling of having lost a part of herself. Slowly she understood that the part which was missing was her "penis" and that her brother's representation symbolized it. This was one of the major reasons behind her complicated mourning reaction.

The transference became "hot" when she identified her therapist as the owner of her "penis." She began accusing him of withholding the "good stuff" from her. She was being "cut off." She stated that speaking of her problems would leave her with a "gaping hole." She befriended a woman whose nickname was identical to her therapist's nickname. By "holding onto" this friend she could feel "undamaged" and powerful. Also she began horseback riding. She chose a special white horse and as she rode him she felt the animal's neck was a powerful phallus between her legs.

Toward the end of the first year of her treatment she came to her therapist's office with a knife in her hand. Giggling, she reassured the therapist that the knife was not intended for him, but for gathering mushrooms; she carried it with her everywhere in case she came across an edible mushroom!

It was through occurrences such as those described above and her understanding the meanings of them that Carol realized how she had transferred her unconscious perceptions and experiences of her sibling representation to the therapist. As she worked through this transference neurosis, Carol began to feel more womanly and to solidify her relationship with her boyfriend. This was followed by the development of an erotic transference to her therapist which also was eventually worked through.

In a dream she saw a man who was "an intruder" to her privacy and she thought of asking her therapist to get rid of this intruder because she was unable to perform this task on her own. Soon she reenacted this dream in real life in the following way.

She visited her parents' home and slept for the first time in the bed that had been Kenny's, awakening during the night with an orgasm after a "dream of masturbation" that reminded her vividly of similar dreams of her teen years. This event, and a "revisitation" of what Kenny had meant to her, was the beginning of her throwing away the disruptive representation of Kenny as an incestuous object and as "their" penis. Soon the patient had a memorable dream: she dreamed of seeing Kenny—looking re-markably like her therapist in appearance and manner—and talking to him. In reply to a question, he told her that from where he had gone he could no longer see what was happening on earth. She hugged him, and sadly told him good-bye.

10 CHARON AND HERAKLES: LIVING WITH A DEAD BROTHER

In Greek mythology the river Styx encircles the underworld where the dead "live." It divides the place of the dead from the place of the living—or links them, depending upon how one looks at it. Hades is the ruler of the underworld; and Cerberus, his vicious dog, guards its gates. The dog is usually described as having three heads, but sometimes as having fifty heads and a snake for a tail. Cerberus welcomes those eligible to enter the underworld, but he prohibits those who do not belong there from entering, and he devours those who try to escape. Charon ferries the dead across the Styx to the underworld. He works under the injunction never to take a living person to the underworld.

Herakles, Greek mythology tells us, had as the last of his twelve tasks to achieve immortality (i.e., to become a god), to catch Cerberus. He demanded that Charon take him in his ferry to the underworld. Frightened by Herakles' look, Charon gave in and took him across the Styx, where Herakles captured Cerberus, the gatekeeper. He took Cerberus with him, up to the land of the living. Later he returned him to the underworld—or the dog

133

escaped, according to another version. To punish him for dis-obeying his rules, Hades chained Charon to the ferry for one year, giving him only one oar to navigate from one bank of the Styx to the other.

Gisela, a 40-year-old single woman who became Dr. Ast's pa-tient, complained early in her treatment that her whole life she had felt as though she, like Charon, was chained to a ferry, end-lessly crossing on muddy water from one side of the river to the other. The association to mud was that it represented depression and that it was the kind in which dead bodies might be preserved forever; and that she could only be released if someone else took over her place. During her analysis Gisela also revealed that at times she had identified with Herakles, too. Like him she had entered the underworld and had faced Cerberus. She constantly felt, at first unconsciously, until her analysis progressed, that she must rescue her dead brother from the underworld.

Gisela had the psychodynamics of a "perennial" mourner (Volkan, 1981; Volkan and Zintl, 1993). The perennial mourner knows that a death has occurred, but behaves as though it has not. The individual is locked in a chronic review of the lost rela-tionship, in an attempt to find some resolution to it. The patient fluctuates between bringing the dead back to life and "killing" the dead to end this mourning process. But the solution never arrives and the patient remains in a state of limbo. We can say that a perennial mourner has a closer relationship with the repre-sentation of the dead than with the representations of living peo-ple. The representation of the dead person becomes a constant companion.

We should add here that this situation may remind us of the concept of twinning (chapter 8) in that there is an excessive preoccupation with a live sibling and his representation. A closer look tells us that in the case of perennial mourning we are not speaking of a twinning phenomenon. The representation of the dead sibling is not utilized to patch up the mourner's sense of self. Furthermore, the patient does not borrow the other's ego functions for performing a mutual task. In the perennial mourner the preoccupation with the representation of the dead is due to the mourner's inability to mourn effectively. The key to analyzing the perennial mourner is to discover what the patient does with the mental representation of the dead person. This mental representation may be externalized. Or it can be internalized: kept within as an object representation separate from, but in a constant and influential relationship with, the self representation.

The perennial mourner sometimes identifies with the mental representation of the dead person. This identification differs markedly, however, from the typical identification seen in individuals suffering from depression following a loss. A depressed mourner identifies *totally* with the object representation of the lost person. Thus the ambivalence felt toward this person becomes an internal clash of love and hate within the mourner. Love drives the mourner to "keep" the mental representation as an identification, and hate drives the individual to "destroy" the mental representation that now has fused with the self representation (Fenichel, 1945). Because of this fusion (identification) the individual turns his hate inward. At best, this lowers self-esteem, and at worst, it leads to suicidal tendencies. Contrary to what we see in depressed individuals, the perennial mourner's identifications with the mental representation of the lost object is temporary and unstable. Identification quickly gives way to differentiation of the object representation from the representation of the self. The perennial mourner experiences low self-esteem and self-hatred temporarily and intermittently. Gisela had the psychodynamics of a perennial mourner, and she also had some aspects of twinning, as we will illustrate. Her experiences in twinning influenced the nature of her perennial mourning.

BACKGROUND

When Gisela was a baby her mother earned extra money as a wet-nurse. Sharing her mother's breasts with another baby might have been the foundation of Gisela's profound sense that she had "no place" of her own in the world. Another aspect of her early life further crystallized her sense of having no place to call her own. Her family was very poor, and shared a small apartment with another family. Gisela, her parents, and her brother Hans, who was five years older than Gisela, all slept in the same room during the first seven years of Gisela's life.

As an adult Gisela could recall the bed her parents slept in, and the little bed her brother had, but she could not recall her own sleeping place. Since she remembered that her brother wet the bed and that she could feel the wetness, she concluded that she must have shared a bed with him. Until her treatment, Gisela had never in her life owned her own bed; she slept in borrowed beds or in her boyfriends' beds. She had never rented a flat or house either. Five months into her treatment with Dr. Ast, Gisela, at the age of 40, bought her first bed.

Gisela had few conscious memories of her early childhood. It became obvious in treatment, however, that trauma around her childhood bedroom arrangement had caused her to develop certain views of life. Besides feeling unentitled to privacy she also experienced certain aspects of twinning with her brother; but in her case, unlike the situation of Mary (chapter 8), easily observable characteristics of twinning did not fully evolve. She must have had some exposure to primal scenes, but she had no conscious awareness of this.

When Gisela was 5 years old, her parents sent her brother, then 11, to a boarding school. The patient recalls feeling agony at that time: "How could they [parents] steal my brother away from me?" When Gisela was 7 years old the family rented an inn as a business venture. After the move her parents had their own bedroom. Hans remained at the boarding school, but when he returned to the inn on weekends and holidays the siblings shared not only a bedroom, but a bed. This kept Gisela's unconscious incestuous and twinning fantasies alive.

Hans continued to wet the bed until he was 12 or 13. This symptom may have reflected the boy's reactions to being forced to live in such close proximity to his parents and sister. From our direct clinical knowledge of other bed-wetters, we know that such a symptom has multiple and condensed meanings, such as expression of anger, defense against anger (putting out a fire with urine) (Freud, 1900), displacing semen to urine (urinating on his sister instead of having sex with her), and defense against incest ("if I pee on you, you won't come close to me!"). In treatment Gisela never reported having actual sexual activities with her brother. If she had such memories, their emerging into consciousness was well defended. She "saw" incest everywhere else, however. For example she felt convinced that her mother and her maternal aunts had been incestuously involved with their father, that her boyfriend once had been his mother's lover, and her brother her mother's lover (at least on a "spiritual" level). At times she thought that her brother was a homosexual and that the priests (fathers) at his religious school were raping him, though she had no actual evidence for these ideas. Her thoughts might have reflected her attempt to protect herself from incestuous impulses: if he were homosexual he would have no interest in her sexually, even if they slept in the same bed!

Whenever he visited the inn, Hans received special treatment. Whereas Gisela worked very hard all week long, Hans did not receive any difficult tasks when he visited. She also had to clean the toilets, and this made her feel ashamed. Her parents made a little money by running the inn, but they often quarreled and sometimes physically abused each other as well as Gisela. At school, she was an average student.

The crowded family living situation had induced in her mind an association to sardines in a can. Her family had often eaten sardines as part of economical dinners. In any case, during her life at the inn her interest in sardines evolved into an interest in Sardinia and Sardinians. She found books about the island and imagined Sardinians, like herself, working very hard every day. She thought that the islanders were cheated in life. They lived on barren land, and they had difficulty in making it produce the fruits and vegetables they needed to survive. She also learned that outsiders had taken the freedom of the Sardinians again and again. The Italians had made "slaves" of them and exploited them, forcing them to pay taxes to their conquering "occupiers." The Sardinians represented her own sense of self as a "slave" at the inn, where the barrenness of her parents' love for her matched the perceived barrenness of the Sardinians' homeland. The twinning with her brother was one means to counteract the lack of emotional nurturing from her parents.

Besides sardines, ants (which also live in crowded quarters) fascinated Gisela. In her daydreams, Gisela reigned as "queen" of the ants. She had heard that the queen ant has no legs, and that other ants have to carry her around and serve her. Her daydream reflected her wish to feel cared for, and to be essential, as the queen, to her nest's survival. It represented her helplessness (no legs) and her need for others. It was also her narcissistic defense (she was a queen).

When Gisela was 11 years old and just beginning to negotiate her adolescent passage, her 16–year-old brother, who had turned into an athletic young man, died suddenly in a skiing accident. Prior to the fatal accident he had experienced "fainting spells" at home and Gisela wondered if such a spell led to his death. During treatment she was vague about the "fainting spells," so we do not know if they were due to biological or biochemical anomalies, if they were conversion symptoms, or if Hans experienced them as a defense against incestuous fantasies.

Gisela recalls feeling happy when she heard of her brother's death. She felt happy because now she would be the sole recipient of her parents' attention, and because she now would have her own room. She wondered if her brother had deliberately killed himself to do her a favor—to give her their room and the full attention of their parents. Part of her happiness about her brother's death might have resulted from her realization that sex between them was now impossible. As we shall explain, her experience of relief at her brother's death overshadowed other, more hidden notions.

After Hans' death Gisela's mother became a sad, bitter, and grieving woman and remained so for many years. A few years after their son's death, her parents divorced. Even though she knew that their divorce made it impossible, Gisela wished that her parents would have another child to replace her dead brother. When Gisela reached age 16, the age of her brother at his death, she became pregnant. It was *she* who would have a baby to replace Hans! As luck would have it, she had a son. With her mother's encouragement, she kept the baby at home. Gisela's mother declared to her now ex-husband, that they had "another Hans."

When little Hans was 6 months old, Gisela took him to a Youth Welfare Department office, where, according to her, the authorities made her sign certain papers, and then "robbed" her of her baby. Gisela also told Dr. Ast that in actuality she had given up the baby for adoption. Following his birth she had experienced increased feelings of being her mother's slave. She felt that she needed to get away from her mother and little Hans, who, even though he reestablished her "twinship," had also given her a reincarnated brother to endure, and who had not served the other purpose she expected of him—to make her mother stop grieving for Hans and become a better mother to her. Instead, after little Hans came along, Gisela became more of a slave, with more tasks to do, and the stress resulted in physical fights between her and her mother that she feared might go too far. Gisela actually worried that one of them might kill the other. With little Hans given to unknown adopted parents, Gisela was free to leave home.

Through her associations to two memorable dreams during treatment, Gisela, in a sense, summarized how she was robbed and left empty during her developmental years. In the first dream a girl who had a pair of beautiful red shoes (representing femininity) is robbed of them. In the second dream an elderly couple (representing parent figures) collected huge mushrooms (penises). She and her brother together took one, but the inside of this mushroom was hollow. This mushroom turned into a small cemetery memorial just like those seen on graves in certain parts of Germany that have a hollow center for inserting flowers or religious icons. In the dream the hollow center was empty. The patient's associations to this dream indicated her unconscious fantasy that when she was involved in a kind of twinning with Hans she could replace her lost femininity by owning his (their) penis. But then, that too was stolen (her brother's death).

At the age of 17, Gisela "fell in love" with a young man she knew to be a thief. He robbed churches and she helped him with some of the robberies. In fact, Gisela had prior experience at thievery, for she had stolen money from her mother. In her treatment it became clear that stealing from her mother and the church (which stood for parents) expressed her sense of "entitlement" (Volkan and Rodgers, 1988). She felt deprived of narcissistic supplies in her childhood and teen years—robbed of her mother's love, robbed of her brother, and robbed of his replacement, little Hans—so she was just taking what was owed to her. She stole candlesticks from the church which stood for phalluses. Her associations in treatment suggested that phalluses stood for her "twin's" penis.

Her boyfriend was not caught but the authorities brought Gisela to justice, sentencing her to a several-year jail term. However, she did not actually stay in prison, but outside, under supervision. Ironically, some thieves she did not know burglarized the inn shortly after her own sentencing. The burglars shot her mother in the back, but eventually she recovered. Gisela moved back into the home after being released on probation. She reported to her analyst that one night she came home late (and failed to be her mother's "slave"), so her mother kicked her out of the house and refused to speak to her for ten years. Finally, the death of Gisela's father forced the mother and daughter to speak together about the funeral and burial arrangement, the details of which we will describe later.

After being kicked out of her mother's home, Gisela lived in an environment where everyone used illegal drugs. During this time she felt like an outsider, perhaps because she seldom used drugs herself, although she did help others inject heroin into their veins. She had a series of boyfriends and consciously wished to change their lives by taking them away from the filth of the city to the clean living of the countryside. None of her affairs lasted very long because she herself would end them as soon as the boyfriend tried to seek a permanent relationship with her; the idea of marrying and having children made Gisela anxious. For each boyfriend she would clean his house or apartment and devote a lot of time and attention to raising flowers and vegetables there (we will explain the importance of these activities later).

Gisela worked at various jobs to earn a living and attended different schools in an effort to upgrade her level of education. This goal produced anxiety in her because her brother had died just before receiving his high school diploma, and it frightened her to approach the same level. At the same time, though, she wanted to achieve earning her (and her brother's) baccalaureate degree.

Five years prior to seeking treatment with Dr. Ast, Gisela lived with a successful businessman who was three years older than her. This man treated Gisela like a child and in her analysis it became clear that he stood for a mother figure. She lived in his apartment and he would shout at her when she did not eat properly. She was his "bad" child, and at the same time she punished him as her "bad" mother. This man had no interest in normal sex. Instead he liked to be tied up and beaten by her. Thus, she had the opportunity to do to her "mother" (parents) what her mother (parents) had done to her.

Then Gisela "fell in love" with a man who was fourteen years *younger*, and two years older than the son she had given up for adoption. During her analysis it was understood that he represented the teenage brother of her childhood and also little Hans, whose whereabouts she did not know. Gisela developed cystitis when she began having sex with this young man. Around the same time, one of her female colleagues attempted suicide, and as a result was crippled for life. These incidents brought Gisela to treatment. We should also mention here that Gisela's new boyfriend was earning money by taking care of graves at a cemetery. He was a cemetery keeper, called a *gardener* in German.

The following is a summary of our understanding of why Gisela came to analysis: Gisela lived with "bad" parents (the businessman) and received their (his) help but had to submit herself to humiliating and unusual sex acts (in the crowded childhood bedroom she must have perceived sex and aggression as intertwined and perverted). In return, she "beat up" her "bad" parents and took revenge. To these psychodynamic processes she added an "incestuous" relationship with her brother/son (the much younger man), and she developed cystitis. Her cystitis related to her identification with her bed-wetting brother, as a defense against incestuous togetherness. It was also a punishment for her unconscious incestuous and aggressive fantasies. When a "death" (her colleague's suicide attempt) occurred, the environment too closely matched that of her younger years, when she had unconsciously wished her brother dead. The reality of the death threatened her ability to restrict her murderous unconscious fantasy to the mental realm. As external reality began to merge with her psychic reality, Gisela became very anxious and sought analysis.

THE BROTHER'S REPRESENTATION AS IT APPEARED IN ANALYSIS

If Gisela's brother had not actually died, Gisela's experiences with his real presence might have altered her mental representation

of him, making it more realistic. Then she might not have preoccupied herself so much with his representation. But because he
did die, she, mostly unconsciously, constantly attempted to "reincarnate" or else to "kill" him. Her brother's death occurred at
the beginning of her "second individuation" (Blos, 1979); because of this her brother's representation became a magnet holding together her childhood self and object images, and her
various impulses and defenses against them. She ambivalently
tried to control this "magnet."

We present the following excerpts from her analysis *sequen-
tially*, as they appeared during her sessions. Some of them more
clearly illuminate her preoccupation with her sibling's representation than do others, but by accumulating the insights of all of
them, we can see a clear illustration of various meanings of the
representation of a dead sibling in a patient's internal world.

First Dream: the Transmigration of Souls

In her very first session with Dr. Ast, Gisela reported that she
knew that the baby she put up for adoption had replaced her
brother. We can surmise that above and beyond external circumstances, she felt ambivalence about the baby (brother). Significantly, after one session with Dr. Ast, Gisela moved into her own
rented apartment. For the first time in her life, she would be the
only tenant, although she expected visits from her young boyfriend. This move, as we understood it later, reflected her wish
to be the only child, and to have privacy. Its meaning formed the
foundation of her first transference reaction toward her analyst.
By her action, in a sense, she declared the aim of coming to
analysis.

Very early in her treatment, Gisela made a slip of the tongue
and referred to her young lover as her son. She also had some
awareness that she had deposited the representations (she called
them "souls") of her dead brother and father into that of her
boyfriend. In her mind their souls intermingled. She referred to
this as "transmigration of souls." She reported a dream of the
"transmigration of souls" in her fourteenth session.

The dream had three parts. The first part centered on two
escalators, side by side, one going up and one going down. She

stood at the bottom of the up escalator, going up, while her father stood at the top of the down escalator, going down. As the steps of the escalator moved and the patient and her father met and passed each other, Gisela said to a female friend who accompanied her, "See, this is my father." When the father reached the bottom of the escalator he bought a subway ticket and disappeared into the darkness.

The second part of the dream contained morgue tables with dead people on top of them. One of the dead people was her father and interestingly enough, his body and face looked young and beautiful, and his eyes were open.

In the third part of her dream she sensed the presence of her father in a room with her, and his presence began to fill up the room. She experienced a pressure on her chest created by her father's presence. She woke up with anxiety, her heart pounding.

Since this dream occurred early in her treatment, Gisela had not yet developed a therapeutic "work ego" (Olinick, 1980, p. 53) which would have allowed her to work analytically with her dream. However, she spoke of her feeling that her dead relatives were not really dead. Relying on the symbols and the manifest content of the dream, the analyst, without informing Gisela (since it would have been premature to share this information until Gisela had developed a working alliance with her), wondered privately about the following meanings of the dream:

The first part might reflect sexual issues. It includes the symbol of escalators (stairs) moving up and down, an image that usually suggests sexual activity (Freud, 1900). The manifest content also introduces her father (sexual/oedipal) to Gisela's (new) female friend, her analyst. The father's disappearance into the subway may symbolize his going into the underworld, to his death. In the second part of the dream the manifest content indicates the merging of her dead father and brother, and perhaps even her lost son. The father's youthful appearance and open eyes indicated that he (father condensed with youthful brother/son) was not really dead for Gisela. And in the third part of the dream the "ghosts" come back—in a way too palpably real for Gisela.

The analyst thought that Gisela's first dream reflected aspects of typical dreams reported by perennial mourners. For example, they typically dream of the dead person in undisguised fashion.

Their dreams often indicate "the illusion that the loss can be reversed; a corpse lies in its coffin sweating profusely or a long-buried body is found to be intact. These dreams reflect a sense that someone pronounced dead is, in fact, alive. They also reflect the mourner's ambivalence; he or she wants the dead to be dead so that [the mourner] can finish grieving, but the dead person lives on" (Volkan and Zintl, 1993, pp. 74–75). By examining the manifest content of the dream in consideration of Gisela's history, Dr. Ast made an initial formulation about Gisela's inner world: Gisela had been exposed to excessive sexual stimulation in a crowded house and bed. Having her privacy intruded upon by others generated frustration in her. Her sexuality and aggression merged, and induced in her an unconscious fantasy that her sexual impulses led to the death of men; but then the interchangeable mental representations of them came back to haunt her. Her fantasy doomed her to a cycle of killing them, reincarnating them, and killing them again. She spent her time ferrying individuals back and forth between the land of the living and the land of the dead, and in this task she identified herself with Charon who was doomed to endlessly cross and re-cross the river Styx, and she also identified with Herakles, who could, through his own will, break through the borders of Hades. In addition, in Greek mythology death and sexuality—the underworld—are intertwined; they intertwined for Gisela too. Gisela's analysis later showed that her analyst's initial formulation was correct.

Spies Everywhere

Soon after reporting her first dream, Gisela developed a paranoid-like ideation. She felt her neighbors were spying on her, especially when her boyfriend visited her and when they were in bed. In reality, she worked as a telephone operator where she had access to private phone conversations and any secrets they might reveal. Now she felt endangered because "they" (the ones she knew secrets about) might suspect her of listening to them, and then kill her in retaliation. She even avoided eating a cake someone brought to work in case it was poisoned.

By developing this paranoidlike condition, Gisela quickly brought her early childhood environment to her sessions. She had slept beside her brother and she feared (at least unconsciously) that her parents knew of her experiences with him. Even though no sex play seems to have taken place, Dr. Ast began to understand that the brother had become an incestuous object to Gisela. During cold weather her mother's suggestion that the children "cuddle together" in the bed to keep warm may have encouraged this and their twinning. Through displacement her brother also represented the oedipal (sexual) father. As a child, in the crowded bedroom Gisela had heard her parents' conversations and activities; she had "spied" on their primal scene activities. Since she had "spied" on them when they had sex, she expected punishment in the form of neighbors (parents) who spied on her when she had sex with her boyfriend/brother/child.

First Christmas

When the first Christmas during Gisela's treatment came, Dr. Ast left for a week-long holiday. During this week Gisela went to the ski resort where her brother had died. She skied, and had the *same* kind of accident that he had had. Luckily, she survived, but she had bruises covering her entire body. She suffered from aches and pains for weeks, during which time she was conscious of her temporary disruptive identification with her brother's representation. Discussing her accident during the sessions after the Christmas holiday led to further understanding of her temporary identification with the dead (or dying) brother.

At the age of 5, Gisela found a bug and noticed a little tree needle stuck in its body. She pulled the tree needle off the insect's body, but realized with shock that she had pulled out one of the bug's legs. Gisela's brother had broken his legs during his fatal accident when he hit the tree. Her memory from age 5 "reached up" and became connected with her brother's death. In the unconscious, time collapses such that the past, present, and future are experienced as one. Freud (1909a) had described this time collapse in the case of his patient, Little Hans. When Little Hans was very young, his mother threatened him with castration, but her threats were nontraumatic to the preoedipal boy. However, once he reached the oedipal age, a reworking of the past transformed a previously nontraumatic event into the child's *present* traumatic reexperience of that event.

The analyst began to think that Gisela's insect story reflected her fantasy that she could kill her brother by castrating him. As Gisela reported the story of the injured bug, she had a sense of "internal bleeding." She could not escape from temporarily identifying (fusing) with her brother.

Soon after this Gisela visited an acquaintance whose family lived in a crowded room; having visitors made the room especially crowded. Gisela noticed that no one paid attention to the children who lived there: a 5–year-old girl and her 8–year-old brother. Gisela became aware that being in this crowded room reminded her of her crowded childhood living quarters. She began to watch the children and she noticed the boy's aggression toward the little girl. This observation brought to her mind memories of her brother's aggression toward her when they were children. Near the home of this acquaintance stood trees whose tops had been "brutally chopped off," and whose trunks were eaten up by worms. Gisela described this scene so graphically that her analyst had a vision of people with their heads cut off. Gisela reported that she wanted to find a way to save these trees, but that she could not imagine how to save them. In the session in which she reported her response to the crowded home and the dead trees, Gisela realized that the "worms" represented her own rage (the German word for "worm," *Wurm,* is spelled like the verb *wurmen,* which means "to anger or to vex"). The visual image of "castrated and mutilated" trees reflected the disfigured body of her dead brother (and her father) which would be eaten up by worms in the grave. She recognized that although she wanted Hans "killed," she was doomed to reincarnate him (her wish to save the trees) in order to complete unfinished psychological business with him.

The Analyst's "Vision"

Gisela's attempt at "reincarnating" her dead brother (condensed with other representations of dead or lost relatives) also appears symbolically in the following story which she told her analyst five months into her analysis. The symbolism appeared in her *analyst's* response to the story as well.

Gisela lived with her former boyfriend, the successful businessman, for five years in an apartment located in a large apartment complex. Her boyfriend's apartment looked out onto a courtyard that had a barren and bleak appearance, and it reminded her of her idea of the countryside of Sardinia. Gisela worked very hard to turn the courtyard into a beautiful herb and flower garden, which attracted insects, bees, and birds. She had created a world where insects would not lose their limbs, but live happily!

Gisela spoke of the "life" in her special garden when she mentioned a neighbor who had received a ring as a gift from her husband after having their son. The neighbor was a happy new mother who was glad to have given birth to a boy. Listening to her patient, the analyst had an unusual experience that startled her. She momentarily had a vision of Gisela being strangled by a cord; the cord in the analyst's vision appeared like a ring around Gisela's neck. Gisela wore a sweater that day, and the neck of the sweater gave the illusion of a cord around Gisela's neck. Curious about this phenomenon, Dr. Ast considered the following: Gisela busied herself turning a barren space into a fertile one, where she "reincarnated" siblings (insects, birds, and flowers), investing them with libido as a new mother (neighbor) invested her son with libido. The patient had split off her aggression and attempted to repress it. During the session the analyst regressed "in the service of the other [patient]" (Olinick, 1980, p. 7) and *she* sensed the existence of split-off aggression. She in turn directed it to Gisela by "hanging" her by the neck.

Easter Eggs

An event at the first Easter of Gisela's analysis gives some insight into her intrapsychic response to holidays connected with Jesus' birth, death, and rebirth. As Easter approached, Gisela planned to paint some eggs and give them as gifts to friends. However, as the eggs boiled, she "inadvertently" fell asleep, and the unattended eggs "burst like a volcano." All the eggs were destroyed. When she spoke of this event later in one of her analytic sessions, it became clear that at Easter, a time of violent death and resurrection, the eggs represented her sibling and her own "destroyed" baby.

The analyst planned to see Gisela on Good Friday prior to her one-week vacation. Gisela "forgot" the time of the appointment and came to the analyst's office at the wrong time. In a sense, she unconsciously "killed" the session and the analyst too. Thinking that it was the analyst who had missed their appointment, Gisela proceeded to a drugstore where she bought a peculiar Easter postcard showing a very ugly Easter bunny with prominent breasts, dressed in a feminine but unattractive dress, grinning and showing her teeth. Gisela wrote a note on the back of the card: "We had a session. I rang four times. You did not open the door. We'll talk about it later. Have a Happy Easter!" She put the postcard into Dr. Ast's mailbox.

After the vacation they analyzed the meaning of the postcard together. The ugly Easter bunny represented the analyst as the "bad" mother onto whom Gisela had projected her (oral) aggression as symbolized by the big teeth of the bunny. The grinning reflected the patient's reaction formation, as did her concluding remark, wishing the analyst a "Happy Easter."

Gisela informed her analyst that after she dropped the postcard into her mailbox, she found herself walking to a nearby cemetery. At the cemetery she became aware of two opposite but simultaneous impulses. The cemetery represented "death." So on one hand she confirmed there the deaths or loss of Hans, her father, her baby, and her analyst. But at the same time, she also felt that the cemetery represented "life," because she saw so many small birds and animals around. She watched them intently. They represented her wish to "reincarnate" the dead. Gisela once more learned about her unconscious fantasies of simultaneous destruction and repair.

Gisela's visit to the cemetery prompted her to tell her analyst the following story about the graves of her brother and father. After her brother's burial, her parents arranged to have a tombstone placed on his grave, with his name, date of birth, and date of death carved on it. The parents planted flowers on the grave, but as time wore on they paid for a cemetery keeper to take care of the grave. The *gardener* (cemetery keeper), then, functioned just as Gisela functioned at her boyfriends' houses. When her parents had less money (or when their investment in their dead child faded), they did not plant new flowers on the grave, but installed a marble stone on it instead. When fifteen years went by without the family paying for the grave's upkeep, the authorities "dissolved" the grave, meaning that the location no longer belonged to the corpse but could be used by new occupants.

Upon the death of her father, Gisela and her mother made a decision to save money by taking the tombstone from Hans' grave and putting it, with newly carved name, and new dates of birth and death onto her father's new grave. Thus, the brother's first name and the dates of his birth and death were erased from the tombstone and the father's first name and dates of birth and death were carved in their place. Gisela's psychological "merging" of representations of two dead people—as was implied in her first dream in analysis which we reported earlier—was carved into stone!

Visit to Sardinia

Fifty days after Easter, at Pentecost, Gisela announced during one of her sessions that she was leaving to go to Sardinia. Without time to analyze her decision, the patient left for the island—the symbolic physical location of Gisela's childhood. She went there to have a kind of "second look" (Novey, 1968) or "pilgrimage" (Poland, 1977). The concept of the "second look" was first described by Novey. He wondered why some patients, during their analyses, have an urge to explore old diaries and papers and to return to the physical settings and persons important to them in an earlier phase of their lives. Novey knew that such activities in some instances constitute "acting out," but "in many more they constitute behaviors in the interest of furthering the collection of affectively charged data and thus helping the treatment process" (p. 87). Novey's ideas are paralleled by Poland's investigation of travels taken to places important in the individual's history.

Upon returning from Sardinia, Gisela reported how she had explored the island, wanting to leave no stone unturned and unexamined. Fifteen years earlier Gisela had seen a movie which was supposedly shot on location in Sardinia. Since we do not know the movie, we do not know if Gisela's recollection matches the movie, or if she modified the story in some way. The following is Gisela's recollection of the movie:

In Sardinia a man and woman who were deeply in love worked on the barren land. The woman became ill and died. The man wanted someone to help him work on the land, so he hired a young woman. She seduced him into having sex with her. Afterward the man strangled the young woman and threw her body into a well. Meanwhile his dead wife rematerialized, sat under a tree and took the life force of a girl passing by, thus allowing herself to look alive. She then found her husband and they lived happily for a few years. Finally one day as they rode their horse along a ravine, the horse collapsed. They all fell into the ravine and died instantly.

Gisela, whose observing ego had developed considerably, tried to understand the impact of this movie on her. She saw a similarity between the couple in love and her "twinship" with her brother. In the movie, seduction and sex (incestuous impulses) cause death. In Gisela's unconscious fantasy, similar impulses caused her brother's death. The movie also included a "reincarnation," just as Gisela wanted to reincarnate her brother, first by having a baby, and then by having a much younger boyfriend. Her unconscious fantasy became a conscious one once she confessed to her analyst her dread that if she found happiness with a boyfriend, he would die.

It seemed that Gisela had done a great deal of psychological work while in Sardinia. Before leaving the island she saw a round, breast-shaped stone lying on the beach. Touching it again and again she found herself soothed and at peace; she thought of it as a magic stone. Although the stone weighed around eighty kilograms, she took it with her to Germany. The analyst suggested that the stone might symbolize a "new object" (new breast/mother/analyst) that Gisela had searched for in order to restructure herself. In the long run, the analyst explained, the magic would not come from this inanimate stone, however, but from finding a solidity within herself.

Later Gisela told her analyst that the stone also represented her budding "new self." The stone was round on top, but flat on the bottom—very stable. When she first saw it, the waves could not move it. "The stone had its own place," she said, and she recalled her aim for seeking analysis: to find her own place in the world and to solidify her own self.

A Sick Breast

Gisela's analysis after she brought the stone to Germany began to include more intrapsychic work on the separation from the representations of lost objects, especially her brother, accompanied by her further individuation from the representation of her mother. During this phase of her analysis the patient began to suffer from a physical ailment in her left breast. She reported that liquid oozed out of her left nipple. No definite diagnosis of her physical condition, however, could be made by the doctors she visited every three months.

By this time in her analysis Gisela was working through aspects of various unconscious fantasies pertaining to her living in a crowded household, a kind of twinning with her brother, incestuous thoughts, and "killing" and "reincarnating" others. We wondered about the existence of an interplay between unconscious fantasies and psychosomatic symptoms (see chapter 1). Did Gisela's beginning to understand the influence of unconscious fantasies on her life lead to her development of psychosomatic symptoms? This is a question we must ask even though we may not give a satisfactory answer to it.

One piece of clinical evidence indicating the possibility of an interplay between the influence of unconscious fantasies and psychosomatic expressions comes from an association Gisela made to her "sick" breast after seeing a movie entitled *A Man Called Horse*. In the film a white man wants to "free" himself from his conventional burdens. He begins to live with American Indians, who put him through a rigorous and painful initiation rite in order to complete his transformation they pierce his breasts with hooks and use them to lift his body into the air. Seeing the character in the movie once more brought Gisela to examine her association of herself with Charon. She felt chained to her brother's representation in her unconscious fantasy as Charon was chained to his ferry. "My breast is my chain," she said. She understood that in her unconscious fantasies she and

Hans not only shared a phallus, but they also shared a connection through her breast, and the unconscious aspects of her twinning were represented in her "sick" breast. Gisela now wished to allow her brother's representation to leave her. However, she wondered who she would be without this representation. She settled on a kind of compromise, by getting rid of only part of Hans.

The Burial of Hans

As the thirtieth anniversary of her brother's death approached, Gisela began mentioning her wish to "bury" Hans (his representation). Gisela now told Dr. Ast that just before his death, Hans had been trying to teach English to his sister, using some of his English school books. Following his death Gisela went to Hans' room and *stole* these English books. Hans' other books, in German, were returned to the school. What she was telling her analyst was that for thirty years Gisela had kept the English books. She was aware of their whereabouts, but she never used them. As the story about the books came up in her analysis, Gisela went skiing on the mountain where her brother had had his accident. There she bought a coin which was minted thirty years ago, in the same year that her brother had died. The books were Gisela's "linking objects," and the coin appeared to be a linking object in the making.

Volkan first described the existence of linking objects of perennial mourners in 1972. Since then he (Volkan, 1981; Volkan and Zintl, 1993) expanded on his understanding of these magical objects. Briefly, a linking object is a physical object that is psychologically contaminated with aspects of the representation of the dead and the representation of the mourner. The mourner typically selects her linking object soon after the death. Then, rather than putting it to its appropriate use—reading a book, or wearing a watch, for example—she will put it in a safe place. Her fantasy (both conscious and unconscious) is that through the utilization of the linking object she can bring back the dead or she can "kill" the dead person and accept the loss. But, she remains in a state of limbo and remains a perennial mourner. Volkan and Zintl (1993) wrote: "We use linking objects to re-create the relationship [with the dead] in the external world, to recapture the vitality and the conflict. Linking objects play the song of the relationship. Ironically, they also keep mourners from adapting and moving on with life" (pp. 80–81). Gisela believed that if she could get rid of her linking objects this would tell her that she now had the ability to break off her relationship with her dead brother. Without first informing Dr. Ast what she planned to do, during the summer of the third year of her analysis, on the Feast of Corpus Christi—the annual celebration of the "Real Presence" of the body of Jesus Christ in the Eucharist—Gisela took the magical books and the coin to a place called *Easterlake*. There she buried the books and the coin. The next day she felt "alive" and well. Dr. Ast, however, noticed the continuation of anxiety in Gisela which she attributed to the magical items being buried at Easterlake which was associated with Easter and, therefore, resurrection; Hans could still return to life.

When Gisela and her analyst spoke about this, Gisela explained that Hans was not yet fully buried, since she had kept her brother's passport with his picture in it, and had not buried it at Easterlake. While Dr. Ast appreciated what kind of internal work enabled Gisela literally to bury her brother's representation—as well as Gisela's corresponding representation linked to Hans' representation—she told her analysand that Gisela's getting rid of the passport would not be the crucial test of her being well. She added that Gisela's task of completing the process of being free of the maladaptive influences of ghosts would take place internally and that they would continue their analytic work to help Gisela accomplish this.

Even after hearing her analyst's words, Gisela was flooded with anxiety. Dr. Ast told Gisela that this anxiety was due to the loosening up of her unconscious twinning, which originally protected her from "bad" affects. Gisela now wanted to complete her individuation. She dreamed of trying to save a sick Hans, but he was doomed to die. She developed a cancer phobia and feared that her "sick" breast would kill her. Part of her wanted to amputate this "sick" breast, while another part of her wanted to avoid this symbolic individuation. She refused, for a time, to see doctors about the breast, and then went doctor-hopping but could not obtain a definite diagnosis. Gisela's case exhibits evidence of the difficulty of completely working through a twinning and the unconscious fantasies pertaining to it. More work will need to be done with Gisela.

11 DIAGNOSIS

Up until now our book may seem to suggest that having siblings is not good for one's mental health! This is, of course, far from the truth. Once more, we would like to remind our readers that our aim in this book is to provide a systematic study of the *psychopathological* residues, in adults, of internalized childhood sibling experiences. The psychoanalytic literature has reported on the benefits of the sibling experience for the individual, across the life span. From the writings of early Freud to the writings of contemporary psychoanalysts, the psychoanalytic literature reflects psychologically or socially adaptive processes that siblings and their representations initiate. For example, Freud (1900) mentioned the help a sibling birth could give to a girl in increasing her "maternal instinct" (p. 252) if the girl is at the right age to respond this way to the birth of a sibling. Freud (1914, 1916–1917, 1921) also mentioned how sibling experiences could initiate learning a sense of fairness and social justice, enhance group feelings, and help the child to connect to a wider world. More recently growth promoting outcomes of childhood sibling experiences have been examined by Parens (1980, 1988), Neubauer (1982), Bank and Kahn (1982), Kris and Ritvo (1983), Provence and Solnit (1983), and Boer and Dunne (1992); and this is by no means a comprehensive list. Abend (1984) and Graham (1988) focus on adult object choice which is based on childhood sibling love. Works such as those presented by Leichtman (1985), Graham (1988), and Sharpe and Rosenblatt (1994) which deal with the siblings' role in the child's developmental struggles, for example, going through separation-individuation or the oedipal phase of the psychosexual development, have opened the door for a new focus on the role of the sibling experience in child development. Reiss (1989) states: "Sibling relationships may be an excellent vehicle for maintaining continuity in social roles and relationships from early childhood through adulthood" (p. 220).

We also see a need for further study of the pathological outcomes in adult patients of childhood sibling experiences. We hope that our book, with its basis in clinical data, and its examination of the pertinent psychoanalytic literature in English of four decades (we also made reference to some key papers published before the 1960s), will inspire others to enhance the field of the psychopathology of sibling relationships. Our reference section should provide guidance for those clinicians who wish to study the internalized sibling experiences further.

OUR PSYCHOANALYTIC TRADITION

In spite of Freud's recognition that childhood sibling experiences play a role in psychopathology as well as in psychological growth (Blum, 1977), it seems to us that as psychoanalysts we have developed a tradition which tends to ignore—in our teaching, in our writings, and most importantly in our practice of psychoanalysis—internalized sibling experiences. Colonna and Newman (1983) state that "sibling" is not mentioned in the index of the *Standard Edition* (although Siberia is), nor is "birth of sibling." "Brothers and sisters" and "relations between" them have five entries. "Nor do brothers, sisters, or siblings appear in the indices of a large number of general texts on psychoanalysis" (p. 285).

In chapter 9 we described the effect of childhood sibling loss on Freud's adulthood. Agger (1988) speculates that Freud's relationships with his siblings were conflictual and that they might have played a role in his minimizing the role of sibling experiences in the formation of psychopathology. Our own clinical experiences and our work with those we have supervised has shown us that analyzing internalized childhood sibling experiences often provides a key to patients' symptoms or personality organizations; and yet, especially among analysts who treat only adults, these issues do not easily come to mind. Graham (1988) described how his own countertransference difficulties interfered at times with his appreciation of sibling representations in his adult patients. He suggested that we should pay more attention to the sibling dynamics both in transference and countertransference. He supported his suggestions with clinical material on sibling relationships that emerged from 35 psychoanalytic cases.

Sharpe and Rosenblatt (1994) stated that the analyst may forget about siblings, not only out of theoretical bias, but because of "countertransference issues related to personal conflicts with siblings" (p. 505). Furthermore, they observed that frequently patients do not mention a crucial sibling even:

> [L]ong after parental issues have been significantly explored. Some patients, in their intense wish to eliminate their siblings or conflictual feelings about them, have succeeded in lulling us into erroneously thinking they are only children. It is possible that the relative paucity of sibling material in reported cases may result from a narrow analytic focus on ferreting out oedipal and pre-oedipal conflicts with parents [p. 505].

Waugaman (1990) described adult patients who avoided referring to a sibling by name. When they finally disclosed the sibling's name this often coincided with the emergence of sibling-related central conflicts in the transference. Such a disclosure also might accompany associations about an earlier intimacy with the sibling which later gave way to subsequent estrangement. Waugaman also notes that in adults' analyses sibling transferences largely have been ignored.

DIAGNOSTIC SESSIONS

The symptoms and personality traits of the patients we have discussed in this book, when they appear in other patients, could alert the clinician to the possible existence of conflicts in adults pertaining to internalized childhood sibling experiences. Other clues may come from the patients' histories. For example, mother's prolonged illness after delivering a sibling, sleeping with a sibling in the same bed regularly during the developmental years, having a deformed sibling, and facing a sibling's death in childhood are events that accompanied conflictual sibling representations in the patients discussed here.

During diagnostic workup with our adult patients the possibility of psychopathology pertaining to sibling representations may manifest itself. The following are three examples. Having already provided extensive analyses of similar cases, we will not explain why we surmise the presence of internalized sibling conflicts from the manifest contents in these examples, but will simply present them as they appeared during diagnostic sessions. In each of these cases the impact of internalized sibling experiences did, in fact, prove to be key factors in the patients' symptoms and pathological personality traits.

Harry

A man in his thirties sought treatment because of severe anxiety which he experienced soon after his brother's wife had a baby. One morning he learned of the baby's arrival when his wife, who had been in touch with her brother-in-law, informed him about this event. That afternoon Harry's brother called him. Harry picked up the phone and heard his brother's voice, but he felt that he could not talk with his brother. Therefore, he hung up the phone. At the same time he had a thought: "Bastard! You should be killed. I'll kill you by hanging up on you!" He was surprised at his reaction. That night his "killing" his brother symbolically became the day residue of a dream.

In the dream Harry was leaning on a covered wagon and wondering, "What is in the wagon?" Then the scene in the dream changed. Harry saw a small, almost naked, bird perched on a branch of a tree. The interesting thing was that the bird began to go through a metamorphosis, becoming bigger and prettier with feathers. But, suddenly, the bird was hit by a "brown thing."

Harry's association to the "brown thing" was that it looked like fecal material (anal aggression). The bird was killed.

For the next few days Harry was determined that he would not go to see the new baby. He kept asking himself, "Why am I so angry at this baby?" without coming up with a satisfactory answer. Soon he had a new dream. In this one he was with a woman who in reality was known as someone who spoke in "baby talk." (She stood for a baby.) In the dream Harry picked up a piece of grass and began masturbating this woman with the grass as if it were a dildo.

Harry was 11 years old when his only sibling, his brother, was born. After the dream he recalled with guilt feelings how he used to masturbate his brother when the latter was still a toddler. His association to grass was that it is destructive to *fertile* flowerbeds and flower seeds (representing a womb and semen).

Anita

Anita's brother was born when she was 3 1/2 years old. Soon after her sibling's birth her maternal grandmother died. Anita felt that she not only lost her mother to her brother but also to grief. Throughout her childhood whenever she heard of a fatal accident she would think that the same tragedy could happen to her sibling. She slept with her brother in the same bed for thirteen years. This apparently affected her personality: she was seductive toward men with whom she felt close, and whenever she dated someone she would automatically compare him with her brother.

In her thirties she went into treatment but there was no analysis of her internalized relationship with her sibling's representation. Instead, she tried to seduce her therapist who in turn would invite her to lunch. The therapeutic position was thus ruined.

After moving to a new city and still feeling uncomfortable with her interpersonal relationships, Anita once more sought treatment. The night before her diagnostic interview she had a dream in which she was opening a door of a cabinet. In the cabinet was a little mouse. A cat appeared and tried to kill the mouse. After reporting this dream Anita spoke of a "funny" habit: she liked to kill bugs; however, she would first bless them before killing them!

Sandra

A woman in her early forties sought treatment just as Christmas was approaching and declared that she hated Christmas. Her reason for seeking treatment was her rejection by her lover of one year, a veterinarian. During the previous Christmas Sandra's dog had been hit by a car and injured. Sandra took the dog to a veterinarian, a divorced man. The veterinarian cured (repaired) the dog. This was very important for Sandra because of her "special relationship" with her dog whose life she "controlled." Whenever Sandra had a new date she would observe the man's relationship with the dog and then she would decide whether to continue to date the man according to the dog's "acceptance" of him.

After the veterinarian cured Sandra's dog she fell in love with him and they began to have sexual relationships. When he rejected her just before the second Christmas of their togetherness, Sandra sought out treatment. During her diagnostic interview she expressed her awareness of her severe childhood sibling rivalry. Her brother was born when she was 2 1/2 years old. In her diagnostic session she said: "My brother took my place and I never forgave him." Sandra was involved in a medical profession which deals with high-risk pregnancies. In a way Sandra was in a position to decide which baby dies and which baby lives by her choice of which medical procedures to initiate. Sandra had never been married and had a conscious fear of pregnancy, but she owned a collection of fetuses in jars (wombs). She kept them for educational reasons, as a teaching tool for students. However, during her diagnostic session she called them "my dead babies"! She had an intense "relationship" with them, but could not explain why this was so.

A SUMMARY OF OUR FINDINGS

The observations of symptoms discussed in this book, if they exist in diagnostic sessions, should alert clinicians to the possibility of internalized sibling experiences in adults which lead to psychopathology. The findings in this book concerning adult psychopathology which derives from interactions with childhood sibling representations in the unconscious have been distilled from seventeen patient cases (5 men and 12 women). We reported some cases only briefly in order to illustrate one or two concepts. For example, Albert's case was briefly summarized in order to demonstrate a disruptive identification with the representation of a sick sibling. Other cases, such as the cases of Lisa, Mira, and Gisela, were described in detail. The full cases, taken together, illustrate in a convincing way a pattern symptoms and observable behavior patterns. Table 11–1 summarizes our observations.

The table indicates the commonality of womb fantasies in those who responded to the representations of younger siblings. Five patients, two men and two women, clearly exhibited claustrophobias. Eight women had fear of pregnancy. Also, in six women, fantasies about pregnancy, delivery, and difficulties relating to siblings created thoughts about sibling/phallus equation or other gender difficulties. Twelve individuals clearly exhibited murderous rage at the representations of their siblings; two of them in childhood actually attempted to murder their baby siblings. One man was involved in an incestuous relationship with one of his younger sisters, and three women exhibited unrepressed incestuous thoughts.

We also reported on one case of replacement child syndrome, two cases of twinning, and seven cases of clear disruptive identifications with sibling representations which led to the formation of symptoms. Christmas or Easter "neurosis" appeared in four cases. Displacement of sibling representations onto animals, birds, fish, and insects also appears very common.

Clearly, we have not amassed enough cases to assign any statistical significance to our findings. The table presented here simply summarizes our clinical experience and supports our premise that siblings in the unconscious can lead to psychopathology in adults. As clinicians we need to pay attention to this phenomenon.

TABLE 11-1. A Summary of Our Findings

	Baby/ Phallus Equation	Displace	Foster or	Murder	Incest or	Replacement

Wash

TABLE 11-1. (*continued*)

Patient/Chapter	Womb Fantasies or Dreams	Claustrophobia	Fear of Pregnancy	Easter or Christmas Neurosis	Displacement onto Animals	Baby/Phallus Equation; Gender Problem	Murder Attempts or Fantasies	Incest or Incest Fantasies	Replacement Child Syndrome	Twinning	Disruptive Identification
WOMEN											
Jennifer 2	+		+			+					
Christine 3	+	+	+		cat	+	+				+
Davis 9	+				h...						

REFERENCES

Abarbanel, J. (1983), The revival of sibling experience during the mother's second pregnancy. *The Psychoanalytic Study of the Child*, 38:353–379. New Haven, CT: Yale University Press.

Abend, S.M. (1984), Sibling love and object choice. *Psychoanal. Quart.*, 53:425–430.

———— (1990), Unconscious fantasies, structural theory, and compromise formation. *J. Amer. Psychoanal. Assn.*, 38:61–73.

Abraham, K. (1911), Giovanni Segantini: A psychoanalytical study. In: *Clinical Papers and Essays*. New York: Basic Books, pp. 210–261.

Agger, E.M. (1988), Psychoanalytic perspectives on sibling relationships. *Psychoanal. Inq.*, 8:3–30.

Ainslie, R.C. (1985), *The Psychology of Twinship*. Lincoln, NE: University of Nebraska Press.

———— Solyom, A.E. (1986), The replacement of the fantastical oedipal child: A disruptive effect of sibling loss on the mother–infant relationship. *Psychoanal. Psychol.*, 3:257–268.

Akhtar, S. & Volkan, V.D., Eds. (in press), *In the Mental Zoo: The Role of Animals in the Human Mind and Its Pathology*. Madison, CT: International Universities Press.

Allen, M.G., Greenspan, S.I., & Pollin, W. (1976), The effect of parental perceptions on early development in twins. *Psychiatry*, 39:65–71.

Apprey, M. (1987), When one dies and another lives: The invariant of unconscious fantasy in response to a destructive maternal projective identification. *J. Melanie Klein Soc.*, 5:18 53.

——— (1993), Dreams of urgent-voluntary errands and transgenerational haunting and transsexualism. In: *Intersubjectivity, Projective Identification, and Otherness*, ed. M. Apprey & H.F. Stein, Pittsburgh, PA: Dusquesne University Press, pp. 102–128.

Ardrey, R. (1973), *The Territorial Imperative: A Personal Inquiry into Animal Origins of Property and Nations*. New York: Atheneum.

Arlow, J. (1960), Fantasy systems in twins. *Psychoanal. Quart.*, 29:175–199.

——— (1969a), Unconscious fantasy and disturbances of conscious experience. *Psychoanal. Quart.*, 38:1–27.

——— (1969b), Fantasy, memory and reality testing. *Psychoanal. Quart.*, 38:28–51.

Bank, S.P., & Kahn, M.D. (1982), *The Sibling Bond*. New York: Basic Books.

Beres, D. (1962), The unconscious fantasy. *Psychoanal. Quart.*, 31:309–328.

Bergman, T., & Wolfe, S. (1971), Observations of the reactions of healthy children their chronically ill siblings. *Bull. Phila. Assn. Psychoanal.*, 21:145–161.

Berman, L.E. (1978), Sibling loss as an organizer of unconscious guilt: A case study. *Psychoanal. Quart.*, 48:568–587.

Binger, C.M. (1973), Childhood leukemia: Emotional impact on siblings. In: *The Child and His Family*, ed. E.J. Anthony & C. Koupernick, New York: Wiley-Interscience, pp. 195–211.

Blos, P. (1979), *The Adolescent Passage*. New York: International Universities Press.

Blum, H.P. (1977), The prototype of preoedipal reconstruction. *J. Amer. Psychoanal. Assn.*, 25:757–785.

——— (1983), Adoptive parents: generative conflict and generational continuity. *The Psychoanalytic Study of the Child*, 38:141–163. New Haven, CT: Yale University Press.

——— Kramer, Y., Richards, A.K., & Richards, A.D., Ed. (1988), *Fantasy, Myth, and Reality: Essays in Honor of Jacob A. Arlow*. Madison, CT: International Universities Press.

Boer, F., & Dunne, J., Eds. (1992), *Children's Sibling Relationships*. Hillsdale, NJ: Erlbaum.

Bornstein, B. (1949), The analysis of a phobic child. *The Psychoanalytic Study of the Child*, 3/4:181–226. New York: International Universities Press.

——— (1953), Fragment of an analysis of an obsessional child. *The Psychoanalytic Study of the Child*, 8:313–332. New York: International Universities Press.

Bowlby, J. (1960), Grief and mourning in infancy and early childhood. *The Psychoanalytic Study of the Child,* 15:9–52. New York: International Universities Press.

———— (1969), *Attachment and Loss,* Vol. 1. New York: Basic Books.

Boyer, L.B. (1955), Christmas "neurosis." *J. Amer. Psychoanal. Assn.,* 3:467–488.

———— (1971), Psychoanalytic technique in the treatment of certain characterological and schizophrenic disorders. *Internat. J. Psycho-Anal.,* 52:67–85.

———— (1979), *Childhood and Folklore.* New York: Library of Psychological Anthropology.

———— (1983), *The Regressed Patient.* New York: Jason Aronson.

———— (1985), Christmas "neurosis" revisited. In: *Depressive States and Their Treatment,* ed. V.D. Volkan. Northvale, NJ: Jason Aronson, pp. 297–316.

Breuer, J., & Freud, S. (1893–1895), Studies on Hysteria. *Standard Edition,* 2. London: Hogath Press, 1955.

Brinich, P.M. (1980), Some potential effects of adoption on self and object representations. *The Psychoanalytic Study of the Child,* 35:107–133. New Haven, CT: Yale University Press.

Burlingham, D. (1952), *Twins.* New York: International Universities Press.

Cain, A.C., & Cain, B.S. (1964), On replacing a child. *J. Amer. Acad. Child Psychiatry,* 3:443–456.

Colonna, A.B. (1981), Success through their own efforts. *The Psychoanalytic Study of the Child,* 36:33–44. New Haven, CT: Yale University Press.

———— Newman, L.M. (1983), The psychoanalytic literature on siblings. *The Psychoanalytic Study of the Child,* 38:285–309. New Haven, CT: Yale University Press.

Dibble, E.D., & Cohen, D. J. (1980), The interplay of biological endowment, early experience, and psychological influence during the first year of life. In: *The Child in His Family,* ed. E.J. Anthony & C. Chiland. New York: Wiley-Interscience, pp. 85–103.

———— ———— (1981), Personality development in identical twins: The first decade of life. *The Psychoanalytic Study of the Child,* 36:45–70. New Haven, CT: Yale University Press.

Dickes, R. (1978), Parents, transitional objects, and childhood fetishes. In: *Between Reality and Fantasy: Transitional Objects and Phenomena,* ed. S.A. Grolnick, L. Barkin, & W. Muensterberger. New York: Jason Aronson, pp. 307–319.

Dowling, S. (1990), Fantasy formation: A child analyst's perspective. *J. Amer. Psychoanal. Assn.,* 38:93–111.

——— Rothstein, A., Eds. (1989), *The Significance of Infant Observational Research for Clinical Work with Children, Adolescents, and Adults*. Madison, CT: International Universities Press.

Eisenbud, J. (1941), Negative reactions to Christmas. *Psychoanal. Quart.,* 10:939–945.

Elbirlik, K. (1980), Open loss, grieving, and itching. *Amer. J. Psychother.,* 24:855–874.

Emde, R. (1988a), Development terminable and interminable. I: Innate and motivational factors from infancy. *Internat. J. Psycho-Anal.,* 69:23–41.

——— (1988b), Development terminable and interminable. II: Recent psychoanalytic theory and therapeutic considerations. *Internat. J. Psycho-Anal.,* 69:283–296.

Fenichel, O. (1945), *The Psychoanalytic Theory of Neurosis*. New York: W.W. Norton.

Freiberg, S. (1959), *The Magic Years*. New York: Scribners.

Freud, A. (1936), The ego and the mechanisms of defense. *The Writings,* Vol. 2. New York: International Universities Press, 1966.

——— (1960), Discussion of Dr. John Bowlby's paper. *The Psychoanalytic Study of the Child,* 15:53–62. New York: International Universities Press.

——— (1965), *Normality and Pathology in Childhood: Assessments of Development. The Writings,* Vol. 6. New York: International Universities Press.

——— Burlingham, D. (1942), *War and Children*. New York: International Universities Press.

Freud, S. (1900), The Interpretation of Dreams. *Standard Edition,* 4&5. London: Hogarth Press, 1953.

———(1905a), Three Essays On the Theory of Sexuality. *Standard Edition,* 7:123–243. London: Hogarth Press, 1953.

——— (1905b), Jokes and Their Relation to the Unconscious. *Standard Edition,* 8. London: Hogarth Press, 1958.

———(1907), Delusions and Dreams in Jensen's *Gradiva. Standard Edition,* 9:1–93. London: Hogarth Press, 1959.

——— (1908a), Hysterical phantasies and their relation to bisexuality. *Standard Edition,* 9:155–166. London: Hogarth Press, 1959.

——— (1908b), On the sexual theories of children. *Standard Edition,* 9:205–226. London: Hogarth Press, 1959.

——— (1909a), Analysis of a phobia in a five-year-old boy. *Standard Edition,* 10:1–147. London: Hogarth Press, 1955.

——— (1909b), Notes upon a case of obsessional neurosis. *Standard Edition,* 10:151–249. London: Hogarth Press, 1955.

—— (1911), Formulations on the two principles of mental functioning. *Standard Edition*, 12:213–226. London: Hogarth Press, 1958.

—— (1914), Some reflections on schoolboy psychology. *Standard Edition*, 13:239–244. London: Hogarth Press, 1955.

—— (1915), The unconscious. *Standard Edition*, 14:159–204. London: Hogarth Press, 1957.

—— (1916–1917), Introductory Lectures on Psycho-Analysis. *Standard Edition*, 15&16. London: Hogarth Press, 1961.

—— (1917a), Mourning and melancholia. *Standard Edition*, 14:237–258. London: Hogarth Press, 1957.

—— (1917b), A childhood recollection from *Dichtung und Wahrheit*. *Standard Edition*, 17:145–156. London: Hogarth Press, 1955.

—— (1918), From the history of an infantile neurosis. *Standard Edition*, 17:1–122. London: Hogarth Press, 1955.

—— (1921), Group Psychology and the Analysis of the Ego. *Standard Edition*, 18:65–143. London: Hogarth Press, 1955.

—— (1926), Inhibitions, Symptoms and Anxiety. *Standard Edition*, 20:75–172. London: Hogarth Press, 1959.

—— (1927), Fetishism. *Standard Edition*, 21:147–157. London: Hogarth Press, 1961.

Furman, R. (1964), Death and the young child. *The Psychoanalytic Study of the Child*, 19:321–333. New York: International Universities Press..

Glenn, J. (1974), Twins in disguise. II: Content, style, and form in plays by twins. *Internat. Rev. Psycho-Anal.*, 1:373–382.

Graham, I. (1988), The sibling object and its transferences: Alternate organizer of the middle field. *Psychoanal. Inq.*, 8:88–107.

Green, N., & Solnit, A.J. (1964), Reactions to the threatened loss of a child: A vulnerable child syndrome. *Pediatrics*, 34:58–66.

Greenspan, S. (1989), *The Development of the Ego: Implications for Personality Theory, Psychopathology, and the Psychotherapeutic Process*. Madison, CT: International Universities Press.

Hamilton, J.W. (1976), Some comments about Freud's conceptualization of the death instinct. *Internat. Rev. Psycho-Anal.*, 3:151–164.

—— (1995), Peter Schaffer's *Amadeus* as a further expression of twinship conflict. *Amer. J. Psychoanal.*, 55:269–277.

Hartmann, H. (1939), *Ego Psychology and the Problems of Adaptation*. New York: International Universities Press, 1958.

—— (1952), Mutual influences in the development of the ego and the id. *The Psychoanalytic Study of the Child*, 7:9–30. New York: International Universities Press.

Hilgard, J.R. (1969), Depressive and psychotic states as anniversaries to sibling death in childhood. In: *Aspects of Depression*, ed. E.S. Shneidman & M.J. Ortega. Boston: Little, Brown, pp. 197–211.

Inderbitzin, L.B., & Levy, S.T. (1990), Unconscious fantasy: A reconsideration of the concept. *J. Amer. Psychoanal. Assn.*, 38:113–130.

Isaacs, S. (1948), The Nature and function of phantasy. In: *Developments in Psycho-Analysis*, ed. M. Klein, P. Heimann, S. Isaacs, & J. Riviere. London: Hogarth Press, 1973, pp. 67–121.

Jacobs, T.J. (1988), On having an adopted sibling: Some psychoanalytic observations. *Internat. Rev. Psycho-Anal.*, 15:25–35.

Jekels, L. (1936), The psychology of the festival of Christmas. *Selected Papers*. New York: International Universities Press, 1952, pp. 142–158.

Joseph, E. (1959), An unusual fantasy in a twin with an inquiry into the nature of fantasy. *Psychoanal. Quart.*, 28:189–206.

Kennedy, H. (1985), Growing up with a handicapped sibling. *The Psychoanalytic Study of the Child*, 40:255–274. New Haven, CT: Yale University Press.

Klein, M. (1948), *Contributions to Psychoanalysis*, 1921–1945. London: Hogarth Press.

Kracke, W.H. (1978), *Force and Persuasion: Leadership in an Amazon Society*. Chicago: University of Chicago Press.

Kris, M., & Ritvo, S. (1983), Parents and siblings. *The Psychoanalytic Study of the Child*, 38:311–324. New Haven, CT: Yale University Press.

Kupfermann, K. (1977), A latency boy's identity as a cat. *The Psychoanalytic Study of the Child*, 32:363–387. New Haven, CT: Yale University Press.

Leaff, L.A. (1984), The psychoanalysis of an individual with a dual developmental trauma: the loss of a parent in the presence of a retarded sibling. *Curr. Issues in Psychoanal. Pract.*, 1:127–140.

Legg, C. & Sherick, I. (1976), The replacement child—A developmental tragedy: Some preliminary comments. *Child Psychiatry & Hum. Develop.*, 7:79–97.

Leichtman, M. (1985), The influence of an older sibling on the separation–individuation process. *The Psychoanalytic Study of the Child*, 40:111–161. New Haven, CT: Yale University Press.

Leowald, H. (1962), Internalization, separation, mourning, and the superego. *Psychoanal. Quart.*, 31:483–504.

Levy, D.M. (1937), *Studies in Sibling Rivalry*. New York: American Orthopsychiatric Association.

Lewin, B.D. (1935), Claustrophobia. *Psychoanal. Quart.*, 4:227–233.

Lidz, T., Fleck, S., Alanen, Y.O., & Cornelison, A.R. (1963), Schizophrenic patients and their siblings. *Psychiatry*, 26:1–18.

————— ————— Cornelison, A.R. (1965), *Schizophrenia and the Family*. New York: International Universities Press.

—— Schafer, S., Fleck, S., Cornelison, A., & Terry, D. (1962), Ego differentiation and schizophrenic symptom formation in identical twins. *J. Amer. Psychoanal. Assn.*, 10:74–90.

Lundberg, S. (1979), Envy and despair in the life of a three-year-old. *Bull. Hampstead Clinic,* 2:3–15.

Mahler, M.S. (1966), Notes on the development of basic moods. In: *Psychoanalysis: A General Psychology,* ed. R.M. Loewenstein, L.M. Newman, M. Schur, & A.J. Solnit. New York: International Universities Press, pp. 152–168.

—— (1968), *On Human Symbiosis and the Vicissitudes of Individuation: Infantile Psychosis.* New York: International Universities Press.

—— Pine, F., & Bergman, A. (1975), *The Psychological Birth of the Human Infant.* New York: Basic Books.

Mintzer, D., Als, H., Tronick, E.Z., & Brazelton, B. (1984), Parenting an infant with a birth defect: The regulation of self-esteem. *The Psychoanalytic Study of the Child,* 39:561–589. New Haven, CT: Yale University Press.

Moore, B.E., & Fine, B.D., Eds. (1990), *Psychoanalytic Terms and Concepts.* New Haven, CT: Yale University Press.

Nagera, H. (1967), *Vincent Van Gogh—A Psychological Study.* London: Allen & Unwin.

—— (1969), The imaginary companion. *The Psychoanalytic Study of the Child,* 24:165–196. New York: International Universities Press.

Neubauer, P.E. (1982), Rivalry, envy, and jealousy. *The Psychoanalytic Study of the Child,* 37:121–142. New Haven, CT: Yale University Press.

Nickman, S.L. (1985), Losses in adoption: The need for dialogue. *The Psychoanalytic Study of the Child,* 40:365–398. New Haven, CT: Yale University Press.

Novick, K.K. (1974), Issues in the analysis of a preschool girl. *The Psychoanalytic Study of the Child,* 29:319–340. New Haven, CT: Yale University Press.

Novey, S. (1968), *The Second Look: The Reconstruction of Personal History in Psychiatry and Psychoanalysis.* Baltimore: Johns Hopkins Press.

Olinick, S.L. (1980), *The Therapeutic Instrument.* New York: Jason Aronson.

Parens, H. (1980), Psychic development during the second and third years of life. In: *Course of Life,* Vol. I, ed. S.I. Greenspan & G.H. Pollock. Bethesda, MD: NIMH, pp. 459–500.

—— (1988), Siblings in early childhood: Some direct observational findings. *Psychoanal. Inq.,* 8:31–50.

Poland, W.S. (1977), Pilgrimage: action and tradition in self-analysis. *J. Amer. Psychoanal. Assn.,* 25:319–416.

Pollock, G.H. (1972), Bertha Pappenheim's pathological mourning: Possible effects of childhood sibling loss. In: *The Mourning-Liberation Process,* Vol. 2. Madison, CT: International Universities Press, 1989, pp. 431–447.

—————— (1973), Bertha Pappenheim: Addendum to her case history. In: *The Mourning-Liberation Process,* Vol. 2. Madison, CT: International Universities Press, 1989, pp. 449–456.

—————— (1989), *The Mourning-Liberation Process,* 2 vols. Madison, CT: International Universities Press.

Poznanski, E.O. (1972), The "replacement child": A saga of unresolved parental grief. *Behav. Pediatrics,* 81:1190–1193.

Provence, S., & Solnit, A.J. (1983), Development-promoting aspects of the sibling-experience. *The Psychoanalytic Study of the Child,* 38:337–351. New Haven, CT: Yale University Press.

Reiss, D. (1989), The represented and practicing family: contrasting visions of family continuity. In: *Relationship Disturbances in Early Childhood: A Developmental Approach,* ed. A.J. Sameroff & R.N. Emde. New York: Basic Books, pp. 191–220.

Ritvo, S., & Solnit, A.J. (1958), Influences of early mother–child interaction on identification process. *The Psychoanalytic Study of the Child,* 13:64–91. New York: International Universities Press.

Rogers, R. (1966), Children's reactions to sibling death. In: *Psychosomatic Medicine.* Proceedings of the First International Congress of the Academy of Psychosomatic Medicine, Spain, Excerta Medica International Congress Series, No. 134.

Rosenfeld, D. (1992), *The Psychotic: Aspects of the Personality.* London: Karnac.

Rosenfeld, H.A. (1965), *Psychotic States: A Psychoanalytical Approach.* London: Hogarth Press.

Rudnytsky, P.L. (1988), Redefining the revenant: Guilt and sibling loss in Guntrip and Freud. *The Psychoanalytic Study of the Child,* 43:423–32. New Haven, CT: Yale University Press.

Sandler, J. (1986), Reality and the stabilizing function of unconscious fantasy. *Bull. Anna Freud Centre,* 9:177–194.

—————— Nagera, H. (1963), Aspects of the metapsychology of fantasy. *The Psychoanalytic Study of the Child,* 18:159–194. New York: International Universities Press.

—————— Sandler, A.-M. (1986), The gyroscopic function of unconscious fantasy. In: *Towards a Comprehensive Model for Schizophrenic Disorders,* ed. D.B. Finesilver. Hillsdale, NJ: Analytic Press, pp. 109–123.

Schafer, R. (1968), *Aspects of Internalization.* New York: International Universities Press.

Segal, H. (1973), *Introduction to the Work of Melanie Klein.* New York: Basic Books.

Settlage, C.F. (1991), On the treatment of preoedipal pathology. In: *Beyond the Symbiotic Orbit,* ed. S. Akhtar & H. Parens. Hillside, NJ: Analytic Press.

Shane, M., & Shane, E. (1990), Unconscious fantasy: Developmental and self-psychological considerations. *J. Amer. Psychoanal. Assn.,* 38:75–92.

Sharpe, S.A., & Rosenblatt, A.D. (1994), Oedipal sibling triangles. *J. Amer. Psychoanal. Assn.,* 42:491–523.

Sherick, I. (1981), The significance of pets for children: Illustrated by a latency-age girl's use of pets in her analysis. *The Psychoanalytic Study of the Child,* 36:193–215. New Haven, CT: Yale University Press.

Slap, J.W., & Saykin, A.J. (1983), The schema: Basic concept in a non-metapsychological model of the mind. *Psychoanal. & Contemp. Thought,* 6:305–325.

Solnit, A.J. (1983), The sibling experience: Introduction. *The Psychoanalytic Study of the Child,* 38:281–284. New Haven, CT: Yale University Press.

—— Stark, M.H. (1961), Mourning and the birth of a defective child. *The Psychoanalytic Study of the Child,* 16:523–537. New York: International Universities Press.

Sperling, M. (1952), Animal phobias in a two-year-old child. *The Psychoanalytic Study of the Child,* 7:115–125. New York: International Universities Press.

—— (1963), Fetishism in children. *Psychoanal. Quart.,* 32:374–392.

Sullivan, H.S. (1962), *Schizophrenia as a Human Process.* New York: W.W. Norton.

Titelman, D., & Nilsson, A. (1992), Are siblings of schizophrenic individuals psychologically disturbed. *Acta Psychiat. Scand.,* 86:411–417.

Trevino, F. (1979), Siblings of handicapped children. *J. Contemp. Soc. Work,* 60:488–493.

Trossman, H. (1990), Transformations of unconscious fantasy in art. *J. Amer. Psychoanal. Assn.,* 38:61–73.

Volkan, V.D. (1972), The linking objects of pathological mourners. *Arch. Gen. Psychiatry,* 27:215–21.

—— (1976), *Primitive Internalized Object Relations: A Clinical Study of Schizophrenic, Borderline, and Narcissistic Patients.* New York: International Universities Press.

—— (1981), *Linking Objects and Linking Phenomena: A Study of the Forms, Symptoms, Metapsychology, and Therapy of Complicated Mourning.* New York: International Universities Press.

———— (1984), *What Do You Get When You Cross a Dandelion with a Rose? The True Story of a Psychoanalysis.* New York: Jason Aronson.

———— (1987), *Six Steps in the Treatment of Borderline Personality Organization.* Northvale, NJ: Jason Aronson.

———— (1995), *The Infantile Psychotic Self and Its Fates: Understanding and Treating Schizophrenics and Other Difficult Patients.* Northvale, NJ: Jason Aronson.

———— Akhtar, S., Eds. (1996), *The Seed of Madness: Constitution, Maternal Environment, and Fantasy in the Organization of the Psychotic Core.* Madison, CT: International Universities Press.

———— Ast, G. (1992), *Eine Borderline Therapie.* Göttingen, Germany: Vanderhoeck & Ruprecht.

———— Ast, G. (1994), *Spektrum des Narzißmus.* Göttingen, Germany: Vandenhoeck & Ruprecht.

———— Greer, W. (1996), True transsexualism. In: *Sexual Derivations,* 3rd ed., ed. I. Rosen. London: Oxford University Press, pp. 158–173.

———— Masri, A. (1989), The development of female transsexualism. *Amer. J. Psychotherapy,* 43:92–107.

———— Rodgers, T., Eds. (1988), *Attitudes of Entitlement: Theoretical and Clinical Issues.* Charlottesville, VA: University Press of Virginia.

———— Zintl, E. (1993), *Life After Loss: The Lessons of Grief.* New York: Charles Scribner's Sons.

Waugaman, R.M. (1990), On patients' disclosure of parents' and siblings' names during treatment. *J. Amer. Psychoanal. Assn.,* 38:167–194.

Weider, H. (1978), Special problems in the psychoanalysis of adopted children. In: *Child Analysis and Child Therapy,* ed. J. Glenn. New York: Jason Aronson, pp. 557–580.

Wolfstein, M. (1969), Loss, rage, and repetition. *The Psychoanalytic Study of the Child,* 24:432–460. New York: International Universities Press.

NAME INDEX

SUBJECT INDEX